Disclaimer

The information included in this book is designed to provide helpful information on the subjects discussed. This book is not meant to be used to diagnose or treat any medical condition. For diagnosis or treatment of any medical problem, consult your own doctor. The author and publisher are not responsible for any specific health or allergy needs that may require medical supervision and are not liable for any damages or negative consequences from any application, action, treatment, or preparation, to anyone reading or following the information in this book. Links may change and any references included are provided for informational purposes only.

Startup

Your Personal Guide For Maximizing Profits, Saving Money, and Doing Things The Right Way With A New Business

By Susan Hollister
Copyright © 2017

Table of Contents

INTRODUCTION 8

CHAPTER 1: THE STARTUP ENTREPRENEUR 10
- Me? An Entrepreneur? 10
- Habits of A Startup Entrepreneur 10
- A Startup, Defined 13

CHAPTER 2: YOUR STARTUP IDEA 14
- Basic Business Types 14
- What is Your Industry? 16
- Clarify Your Idea 17
- What's Your Business Category? 18
- Start With Your Passions 19
- How Good's Your Idea? 20
- The Feasibility Report 20
- Know Your Market 21
- Your Financing Overview 22
- Other Considerations 22

CHAPTER 3: BRINGING YOUR IDEA TO LIFE 24
- Visualize It 24
- Resources 24
- Choosing Your Allies 25
- Organizational Structure 29
- Legal Structure 30
- A sole proprietorship 30
- A partnership 31
- Limited liability companies 31
- Set Goals and Deadlines 32
- Hold Yourself Accountable 32
- Build and Test a Prototype 33

CHAPTER 4: THE IMPORTANCE OF A BUSINESS PLAN 34

- The Executive Summary 34
- Startup Description 35
- Products and Services 36
- Industry Outlook And Market Analysis 36
- Describing Your Operations 37
- Management Team 37
- Analyzing Your Competition 38
- Marketing Strategy 38
- Financial Plan 38
- Writing Your Business Plan 39
- The Overall Structure 40
- Plan Maintenance 40
- Review Planning 41

CHAPTER 5: NAMING YOUR STARTUP 42

- Know What You Stand For 42
- Know To Whom You Speak 42
- Short, Memorable, and Pithy 42
- Domain-Name Friendly 43
- SEO Is Your Friend 43
- Researching Keywords 44
- Names to Avoid 44
- Is It Legal? 45
- Solicit Feedback 45
- Naming Tips 46
- Welcoming Improvements 47

CHAPTER 6: PUTTING YOUR STARTUP ON THE MAP 48

- General Considerations 48
- Accessibility 49

FINANCIAL CONSIDERATIONS 49
DOES IT SUPPORT YOUR BRAND? 49
HOW CLOSE IS THE COMPETITION 50
HOW CLOSE ARE YOU TO SUPPLIERS? 51
VISIBILITY 52
THE SAFETY ANGLE 53
SOUNDNESS OF THE PROPERTY 53
LEGALITIES TO CONSIDER 54
HELP WITH PESKY DETAILS 55

CHAPTER 7: YOUR MARKETING AND BRANDING STRATEGY 57

MARKET YOUR EXPERTISE 57
PROBLEM-SOLVING FOR YOUR TARGET AUDIENCE 58
WHAT ARE YOU REALLY SELLING? 58
YOUR IDEAL CLIENT PROFILE 59
MARKET TO THEIR MOTIVATIONS 60
SERVE YOUR CUSTOMERS 60
YOUR MARKETING STRATEGY 62
MARKETING STRATEGY DESIGN 62
DEVELOPING A MARKETING BUDGET 63
MARKETING PLAN DESIGN 63
SWOT ANALYSIS 64
THE FOUR PS 64
MARKETING METHODS 66
PUTTING IT ALL TOGETHER 68
YOUR BRAND STRATEGY 68
ANALYZING YOUR MARKETING EFFECTIVENESS 69
BRANDING STRATEGY 70
BRAND LOYALTY AND BRAND EQUITY 70
REVIEW CUSTOMER BENEFITS 71
ALIGN WITH CUSTOMER VALUES 72
SETTING BRAND OBJECTIVES 72

SET GOALS TO SUPPORT YOUR MARKETING OBJECTIVES......... 73
MULTIPLE BRANDING 75
REVISIT AND TWEAK 75
BUSINESS DEVELOPMENT STRATEGY.................................. 76

CHAPTER 8: BUILDING YOUR STARTUP TEAM . 79

LETTING GO 79
STRUCTURING YOUR BUSINESS TEAM 80
WHICH OFFICES DO YOU NEED?.. 82
EXPANDING YOUR TEAM 83
TIPS FOR BUILDING STARTUP TEAMS 84
CREATING AN ADVISORY BOARD 86
QUALITIES TO LOOK FOR 87
COMMITMENT LEVEL... 88

CHAPTER 9: YOUR CUSTOMER SERVICE STRATEGY 90

PERSONALIZE YOUR INTERACTIONS 91
BUILDING A GREAT CUSTOMER SERVICE TEAM 92
IMPORTANT CUSTOMER SERVICE TIPS................................. 94

CHAPTER 10: COMMON LEGAL ISSUES FOR STARTUPS... 99

INTERNAL LEGALITIES 99
EXTERNAL LEGALITIES 101
TYPES OF BUSINESS INSURANCE 103
INTELLECTUAL PROPERTY 105
INTELLECTUAL PROPERTY STRATEGY 108

CHAPTER 11: FUNDING YOUR VENTURE 109

LOANS AND CREDIT LINES... 109
INVESTORS 109
CROWDFUNDING 110
BOOTSTRAPPING 111

- Grant Funding 111
- Other Resources 112
- Local Organizations 112
- Space Sharing 113
- Bartering 113
- Self-Funding 114

CHAPTER 12: FINANCIAL PLANNING 115
- The Start Of A Budget 115
- Tracking Your Costs 115
- Expense Categories 116
- Sales Forecasting 117
- Startup Costs 118
- Income Statement 119
- Balance Sheet 120
- Cash Flow Report 120

CHAPTER 13: PREPARING TO LAUNCH 122
- Pre-Launch Checklist 122
- The Press Release 123
- Publishing Your Press Release 124
- Email Announcements 125

CONCLUSION 126

MY OTHER BOOKS 129

Introduction

So you have a great idea for a new business or want to find the right business to start that is best for you. Well, you have made a smart decision in purchasing this book. Too many people don't take the time or effort to properly research what they are doing, and that is why so many new businesses fail. It is much smarter to plan and discover what you are getting into rather than walking into the jungle blindly.

When a business is brand new, it offers a brand new product or service or offers an existing product or service in a new way. Startups have the potential to become incredibly profitable but are also very high risk because when you introduce a new idea to the market, there is no immediate way to measure its success until it launches and tests the market for itself. The founder(s) of the startup often begin running it by themselves until it is time to expand and bring on more team members to take over the show so the founders can work on the business rather than in it.

Although launching a startup can be high-risk and tricky to run, doing it the right way can open the possibilities of massive success and the ability to be your own boss. A startup can start out in your home or between you and some friends and quickly spiral into a well-known name in its industry. Startups are launching every day. Some of the newest and most recent startups that are quickly gaining popularity are DropBox, AirBnB and SnapChat, all of which you are already likely familiar with due to their own success. As successful as these examples are, launching a startup that grows into success can be very difficult.

In this book, you will discover how to cover all of your bases and do everything the right way when launching a startup of your own. Since startups are tend to be very risky, you will definitely want to know how to get set up correctly the first time around so you don't make the same mistakes tens of thousands of people have done before you.

In the following pages you will learn how to create a startup that stands the best chance of success. You will discover what it means to be a startup entrepreneur and how you can utilize certain strategies, skills and habits to do things the right way the first time. You will also learn how to come up with and research a solid startup idea if you haven't already done so. You will then discover the best ways on how to bring your idea to life as a thriving and profitable business.

Chapter 1: The Startup Entrepreneur

When you are a business owner you are also an entrepreneur. An entrepreneur operates or is involved with a business's operations. Startup entrepreneurs are innovative business owners who often capitalize upon new trends and opportunities, so they can provide something new to the world or offer it in a new way. They are also willing to take risks Their main objective is to earn as much money as their talents allow.

Me? An Entrepreneur?

You do not need a college degree or any special training to be a startup entrepreneur. In fact, some of the most famous and successful entrepreneurs dropped out of school (although I do not encourage this!). The example of people like Andrew Carnegie and Mark Ecko shows that anyone can be an entrepreneur; you just need enough drive and the motivation to carry you through.

Are you an entrepreneur by nature? If you don't think you are, there's no need to worry. Some people are more naturally suited to become entrepreneurs, but anyone who really wants it enough can undoubtedly become one!

Habits of A Startup Entrepreneur

Here are some traits commonly found in entrepreneurial individuals:

- You have a roaring, insatiable, and creative mind – you are constantly doing and creating. You're always coming up with and exploring new ideas and fresh ways of doing things.

- You dream big and are willing to do whatever it takes to make those dreams come true.

- You can easily identify a flawed idea when you see one.

- You constantly think of ways to make things better and you generally want to help others.

- You want to do the right thing.

- You have a well-disciplined mind.

- You don't like taking orders from others; you'd rather be in charge of things.

- You reflect on your experiences and look for "lessons learned" so you can improve yourself.

- You're naturally open to learning new things and discovering fresh perspectives for things you already know.

- You enjoy getting an early start to your day so you can get more accomplished; You tend to go to bed at the same time every night.

- You're most interested in *how* existing businesses function; you want to probe their inner workings.

- You're not discouraged by constructive criticism; you are open and highly responsive to feedback.

- You stand up to adversity and do not let any challenge or roadblock get in the way of reaching your goals. You also recognize the value and reward of hard work. You constantly seek challenges.

- You're able to accurately identify your strengths and you know and admit to your weaknesses.

- You enjoy setting goals and creating daily routines. You set yourself a deadline for each goal you are pursuing.

- You exercise and maintain a healthy diet to keep your mind and body in peak condition, so that you can work productively.

- You embrace risk and you're not afraid of meeting new people.

- You have highly disciplined time management skills. Others can set their watch by you.

- You don't let failure discourage you or hold you back. You're passionate about making your dreams come true, regardless of any obstacles you encounter.

- You ask the right questions, questions that will equip you to get ahead.

- You're a planner; you always have to have a plan for your day.

- You're a delegator; you know the perfect people and trust them to help with your plan.

- You're a competitor; you prefer to be in the lead.

- You have the ability to say "no" to things you're not comfortable with or things you believe are a waste of your time.

- You can see the potential in other people and work to help them be successful.

- You respect others, regardless of their personality, culture, or beliefs.

- You're confident in your skills and abilities.

- You remain calm in adverse situations and are able to make decisions based on logic and facts, rather than emotions.

A Startup, Defined

A startup is a business that starts out new and small, but has the potential to become highly successful. Startup entrepreneurs often launch a business in hopes of providing a new product or service that can help others, regardless of how much – or little – money it will generate. Frequently, a startup will exist for a couple of years before it begins to gain a reputation, let alone generate a profit. While the goal of a startup entrepreneur may not be initially to make tons of money, a startup entrepreneur usually holds a vision of his or her business idea eventually dominating the market.

A new business is usually considered a startup for the first three to five years, or until it merges with another larger company, expands to an additional location, gains more than 75 employees, and/or has generated a significant profit.

Chapter 2: Your Startup Idea

There are many types of businesses you can create, but some are especially popular options as startups. The great thing about starting your own business is that there are many industries from which to choose. Each type of business has its advantages and disadvantages. Some, most notably sales ventures, will require you to have more experience than others before you can become profitable. Some businesses require little to no money to start, while others will demand considerable capital up front. However, with the right amount of motivation, determination, and research, you can build a profitable business in any industry.

Basic Business Types

Retail businesses generally operate a storefront to sell products. Examples of retail businesses are clothing stores, book stores, jewelry stores, cell phone stores, etc. Retail businesses can also exist as online storefronts. There are many easy ways to set up your own online storefront through services such as PayPal and Shopify. You can also sell via a third-party online storefront, such as Craigslist or eBay.

Wholesale businesses allow you to buy large quantities of products directly from manufacturers to sell to smaller retail shops. For example, a wholesaler may sell a certain brand of soda products to a grocery store or a certain line of pastries to a restaurant. These retailers then turn around and sell the products to their customers.

Franchises are what you buy when you purchase a <u>license</u> to sell products or services owned by an established, existing company. Fast-food restaurants are a popular type of franchise. Entrepreneurs will often buy a group of restaurants from a single franchise so they can operate in multiple locations. While franchises can be very profitable and highly successful, owners must often pay franchise fees and royalties to the franchisor and abide by specific terms set by the franchising company.

Service-specific businesses are attractive as startup companies, because they do not require as much launch funding as other business types. You can often work for yourself if you're a skilled expert in a given field. Freelance writing, construction, and financial consulting are some of the most popular service-specific business types. Expert professionals, such as doctors, dentists, and lawyers are also considered service businesses. Sometimes a service-specific business will also fall into the sales category. For example, a dentist may offer top-of-the-line toothbrushes for sale, in addition to providing dental services.

Digital businesses are popular as startups because they tend to require the least amount of money to start and will require little more than the use of a computer with internet access. Many freelancing businesses fall into this category. Any type of service that can be performed from a remote location is considered a digital business.

***Assembly*-based** services also make for great startup companies. In this type of business, a person or team of people will subcontract projects from larger manufacturing companies. They will assemble, package, or otherwise combine a product that is already in existence, for final sale.

Sales businesses that sell makeup or clothing products through reputable companies like Avon or Posh are another startup option. Your line of products and your target audience may be somewhat constrained by the type of product you're selling. If you're good at arts and crafts, selling your own creations can provide another profitable option. Many artists and craftsmen sell personalized mugs, t-shirts, jewelry, and other accessories through brick-and-mortar and online sales platforms.

Remember, a startup is either a business that sells a brand new product or one that offers an existing product or service in a brand new way. It's important that you avoid copying an already existing business idea. Your idea must be different enough from everything else in the market that it qualifies as a new idea.

What is Your Industry?

Your industry is basically a way of classifying your business. There are several reasons you should know your industry inside-out. First, it gives you an industry profile that will help define your business within that industry. An industry profile provides key information about the industry you are entering. It includes a forecast of where your type of business will be headed in the future. This information helps you make smart decisions about the viability of your business idea. Before you commit to this specific idea, you will want to research the related industry to determine if the business is even worth pursuing.

The list of industries is fairly standard. The main categories consist of:

- Agricultural businesses.

- Business services.

- Consumer service businesses.

- Education-based businesses.

- Energy and utility businesses.

- Entertainment businesses.

- Financial-based businesses.

- Healthcare-based businesses.

- Manufacturing businesses.

- Non-profits.

- Real estate and construction businesses.

- Retail businesses.

- Technology-based businesses.

- Telecommunications.

- Transportation businesses.

- Travel businesses.

- Wholesaling.

For example, a networking service business would fall under the classification of business services. If you wanted to start a limousine company, your industry would be transportation. If you wanted to sell your hand-made jewelry it would fall under a retail classification.

Once you've narrowed down your business type, you will want to research that specific industry to determine if your idea has the potential for a successful launch and a profitable lifetime within that industry.

Clarify Your Idea

After you have familiarized yourself with your chosen industry, the next step is to clarify your startup idea, if you haven't already. The possibilities for startup ideas are endless. It may take some research and time to come up with an idea that is unique, but your work will be worth it; all of your research will only add to your knowledge of your chosen industry.

Take the time to consider items that are currently trending, especially with a technology-based business idea. For example, you wouldn't start a business selling a new cassette tape player in the year 2017! However, if you wanted to start a video-streaming service that also downloads the videos to your television, this might be a viable option.

To keep on top of the wave of current trends, you'll also want to consider what streaming services and television technology will look like over the next five to 10 years. You're looking for an idea that will succeed not just in today's market but over the long-haul. It must be able to be changed, upgraded, and restyled to follow shifts in industry focus and popular trends.

What's Your Business Category?

If you've already settled on your startup idea and have researched it to test its feasibility in the market, congratulations, you're a step ahead of the game! Feel free to skip this section.

However, if you have not settled on a viable idea, or if you want some help thinking through all important aspects of your business idea, this section should be of help. While you probably won't come up with a fully developed concept overnight, here are some business categories that are promising. Delve into what interests you and work through it until you have come up with a unique startup venture:

- Application software.

- Box delivery businesses.

- Cleaning services.

- Consulting or coaching.

- Contractor or handyman.

- Electronics repair

- Food-based ideas.

- Freelancing.

- Gardening and landscaping services.
- Health and nutritional services.
- In-home services.
- Instructor.
- Kid-friendly products or services.
- Pet services.
- Photography.
- Researching.
- Social media based businesses.
- Tour guiding.
- Translation.

These are just some ideas to help get your creativity flowing – the possibilities for new businesses are endless.

Start With Your Passions

In my experience, I've discovered that some of the best business ideas, literally come out of nowhere. In addition, some of the very best ideas are surprisingly simple! You may want to play the "what-if" game, asking yourself questions to spark a new idea. Keep your eyes open when you're out and about; look for ways to improve existing products or services. Try to find a need that is just crying out to be filled.

Include your talents and passions when you brainstorm. If you can identify a talent or passion and find a way to make it your life's calling, you are more likely to experience success and happiness as an entrepreneur. It's easier to succeed when you're working within areas of interest and desire. When you do for a living something you love and are passionate about, it's a hundred times easier to motivate yourself to get up every day and keep working until it pays off!

How Good's Your Idea?

Once you've come up with a really great startup idea, you will need to prove that it has the ability to be profitable. Your amazing idea just may be too far ahead of its time. You may discover that the capital requirements are too costly right now to make it a profitable venture.

You'll want to test the feasibility of your idea. A friend of mine once came up with an idea to invent car windshields that would turn dark when in contact with the sun; it's an idea similar to light-sensitive eyeglasses. Unfortunately, he soon discovered that it would be too expensive to manufacture. He also learned it would conflict with the states that have regulations prohibiting tinted car windows.

I suppose you're wondering exactly how you can determine if your business idea is feasible. Well, that's why we have the feasibility report.

The Feasibility Report

One of the best ways to test the viability of your great idea is to research and prepare a feasibility report. The feasibility report will provide an overview of your business idea, and describe your chosen market. It will help you estimate the finances you will need to turn your idea into a sellable product. This report will take into consideration issues such as whether you have the necessary skills to successfully bring your idea from initial concept to reality. It also will note any governmental regulations that could stand in your way and will describe what it will take to overcome them.

This information will put you a step ahead when it comes time to write your business plan and will also help you when you set out to pursue financing. We'll discuss these activities in future chapters, but for now, it's enough to know that a highly detailed, thoroughly researched, and well-thought-through feasibility report will be worth your efforts. If the numbers work out and everything makes sense, you'll already be a step ahead when it comes time to create your actual business plan.

In the beginning of your feasibility report, it is important to briefly describe your potential business idea. Include what will make it stand out from similar existing items. Next, list each of your initial products and services and in a couple of sentences describe each one accurately. Then, you can focus on these sections of the report:

Know Your Market

Under the market section of your feasibility report, you should be able to answer the following questions:

- Is there a demand for my product or service?

- Does my industry analysis look promising?

- Who is my target market audience?

- How can I eventually expand my target audience?

- How does my product or service stand out from the crowd? Why will my target market audience want to buy from me?

- Who are my competitors? What advantages do they have over me? What advantages do I have over them?

- What other marketing obstacles do I need to consider?

Your Financing Overview

Under the finances section of your feasibility report, you will answer the following questions:

- How much capital do I need to get this off the ground?

- How easy will it be to acquire capital?

- How will I finance my business during its initial stages?

- What are my fixed costs? My variable costs?

- How many products or services per customer do I expect to sell?

- Will I be able to make a profit?

- How much will it cost to increase my customer base?

- What is the pricing strategy for my products and/or services?

- What does my sales forecast look like?

- How promising is my return on investment?

Other Considerations

This section of your feasibility report will include more factors that have the potential to impact your profitability. Here you will want to include descriptions of the following:

- Location.

- Required licenses and permits.

- Intellectual property rights.

- Regulatory requirements.

- Necessary skills and training.

- Hiring needs and availability.

- Changing trends.

- Anything else you can think of that pertains to the feasibility of your business.

After you've created your feasibility report, you'll want to read it back to yourself. Do the data show that your new idea has the possibility of surmounting the all risks and obstacles to become profitable? Will it be able to withstand the test of time?

If the information in this report indicates that success is probable, you have a viable business idea on your hands! If something doesn't match up or the numbers don't reflect sufficient growth potential, you may need to revamp your idea or select a new one altogether.

Chapter 3: Bringing Your Idea to Life

At this point in your journey you should now have a feasible startup business idea and be ready to bring it to life. It's very important to be realistic with yourself when considering the ideas provided in this chapter. Otherwise, your business may not stand a chance when you transfer it to the real world.

Visualize It

In my experience, I have found that the art of visualization is a powerful technique to help bring any idea to life. Visualization is the act of mentally imagining yourself stepping through the process of successfully reaching an objective. The more you practice visualization and the more details you can build into your mental picture, the more likely you are to be successful at achieving it in reality. When you visualize your dreams daily, it motivates you to take initiative that will eventually lead to the results you want.

If you've chosen an idea that the numbers show can be successful, and if it's something you're passionate about, you've probably been practicing visualization already, without even thinking about it. To visualize your dreams most effectively, include all of your five senses – sight, sound, touch, taste, and smell. Imagine what your product, office, or logo will look like when everything is up and running. Visualize yourself hearing impressive feedback from your customers and receiving constructive criticism that will make your product even more successful! Imagine every detail to make your visualization experience amazing. The more detailed you are, the more likely you will be to achieve success.

Resources

To bring your idea to life, you should identify the resources necessary to launch your business. You'll want to list these resources in preparation for the day you will need to make an expense list for your financial plan.

While you're visualizing your successful business operations, pay close attention to each item you use in the process of creating your product or setting up your service. These are the resources, or expenses, you will need to include in your resource list.

Can you run your business out of your home or will you need to rent office space? Your business location is an essential resource, so include it first in your resource list.

Can you manufacture your products using simple items you can buy in a craft shop, or will you need to bulk order high quality raw materials? You'll want to include each detail in your list.

Next, you will take your resource list and research the cost of each item. Yes, it will take time, but the more accurate your cost analysis, the better you will be able to realistically predict all other aspects of your business. You'll want to check several suppliers, banks, real estate agencies, and other sources to first gain a ballpark figure; then you can pursue the best possible deals for each resource. Even if you don't start spending money right away, your research will help you formulate an accurate startup budget.

Choosing Your Allies

Things can quickly become overwhelming in the business world, especially for first-time startup entrepreneurs. If you've never experienced full autonomy at work or known what it's like to run a business all by yourself, you're in for some pretty big changes to your life. What can save you is the knowledge that you don't have to go through this alone.

There are <u>four key allies</u> who can help to ensure that you have a great experience during the early days of your startup. These allies consist of your mentor, your lawyer, your accountant, and your banker. Having at least one ally in each of these categories can go a long way toward smoothing your path. It also shows potential investors that while you may not be an experienced entrepreneur, you have solid advisors working with you.

Mentor

An experienced business mentor can be especially helpful for first-time startup entrepreneurs. A mentor is someone you can turn to for feedback. Your mentor can serve as a sounding board; a mentor's experience and wisdom can prove invaluable as you delve into the uncharted territory (for you) of starting a business. Mentors are the perfect allies for those times you run head-on into a challenge and you have no idea where to turn next.

A mentor can be a great source of moral support when it comes to launching your first startup. I was lucky enough to meet the woman who became my business mentor during my internship, but if a mentor doesn't fall into your lap, here are some ideas that may help you find one:

- Network, network, network. Put yourself in social situations that lend themselves to meeting other like-minded entrepreneurs.

- My dad always told me the best way to get someone to talk to you is to offer to buy them a cup of coffee. Offer a promising potential mentor a cup of joe in exchange for answering a few business-related questions.

- Make yourself visible to other business owners by attending workshops and seminars and by introducing yourself to other attendees.

- Use LinkedIn to look for potential advisors. For example, if you want to launch a software startup, you can go to LinkedIn and use the search function to locate somebody in your area with a software and business background. Then, fire off an introductory email explaining your situation and asking if they'd be open to consider serving as your mentor.

How to Build a Mentorship

Even if you've found somebody to be your mentor, you cannot expect the mentorship to blossom overnight. Like any other human relationship, the bond with your business mentor will take time to develop and will require work to maintain.

You'll want to be sure the person you've picked has enough time to devote to mentoring you. Business owners tend to be short on time. If you can't get your prospective mentor to meet with you for a measly half hour a week, you may need to look for someone else.

Once you've found the right match, both of you should agree on how often you'll meet, how many meetings you'll commit to for this first period, and what topics you'll be covering together. Even after the formal period of meeting together is completed, you may be able to interact less frequently, although I find that business mentors often become friends for life.

Lawyer

It may come as a surprise that you will need a lawyer to enter into any kind of business. I didn't even think of a lawyer when I launched my first sole proprietorship, but a couple of years later, I discovered why having one is so important. An attorney with knowledge of business law will be able to advise you on everything from the trademarking of your business name to whether or not you can legally run a business out of the location you've selected.

There are many laws surrounding the digital side of your startup. An attorney can help you with the wording of your privacy policy and the terms of use page on your company website. Both of these are demanded by law and require very specific wording.

It will also be to your benefit to have a business lawyer in place, in the event of a lawsuit or other legal action associated with your business. You'll want to face any legal challenges with an expert by your side who knows the law and is thoroughly familiar with your business.

An attorney in your pocket is also great preventative medicine. Many first-time startup entrepreneurs make the beginner's mistake of procuring the services of a lawyer only *after* a lawsuit is filed against them. The problem with signing on a lawyer after the fact is that you probably missed the opportunity to prevent the lawsuit from occurring in the first place. Now, you're responsible for the resolution of the problem, which will likely cost you a pretty penny. Had you put that money toward a lawyer in the first place, your legal counsel may have been able head off potential disaster by pointing out ahead of time the problem that has gotten you into hot legal water. A quality attorney will also advise ways to remedy a potential disaster *before* problems can arise.

When you are searching for a lawyer, you will discover there are certain important factors to consider. The majority of business lawyers specialize in specific areas of business law and their fees vary widely. Larger law firms are able to provide excellent lawyers who can specialize in multiple areas of business law, offering you amazing protection. In addition to providing protection from potential lawsuits, business lawyers can help you navigate the waters of contracts, zoning issues, licenses/permits, copyrights, trademarks, and intellectual property.

Accountant

If there's one thing you should never attempt by yourself in the world of business, it's your taxes. Personal taxes can be confusing enough if you aren't an accountant. As you will soon discover however, businesses are taxed differently than individuals. The tax calculations for a business are much more complicated, so it's best to leave this part of your business to the professionals. Then you will be free to focus on what you do best, the successful running of your business.

In addition to helping you pay your business taxes, your accountant can help you with your financial statements, balancing your books, and planning for future taxes, all of which are basic to successful financial planning. We'll talk about this in greater detail, toward the end of this book.

When your startup is small you may be able to handle most matters yourself if you have some knowledge of taxes. If you hire a tax consultant to guide you, you can save a little money, initially. A sole proprietor can usually learn how to send in estimated tax payments to the government, since this is pretty much all that is required of that type of business. However, as your startup grows and your legal structure develops, I can't emphasize strongly enough the importance of hiring an accountant to handle tax matters for you. It's easy to fall into legal trouble if everything isn't done the right way the first time around, so in the end, paying an accountant will be worth every cent.

Banker

Again, you may be thinking that having your own banker for business matters is unnecessary, but a banker can actually be a useful ally. You may initially need only a separate checking account or help applying for a business loan. In the long run, however, a banker can simplify matters for you. You may start out with no need for payroll arrangements, but when you begin to add staff, your banker is the person who can help you set up accounts to best manage your affairs. A trusted banker who knows your business can also serve as a financial advisor, helping you avoid potential pitfalls and explaining ways to anticipate and manage various business challenges.

Organizational Structure

Before you delve into determining your legal structure, it can be helpful to consider your organizational structure. Your organizational structure will reflect how your operations flow from founders to employees and everyone in between.

First, you want to ask yourself, "Who is involved in the business?" Are you the sole owner and operator? Are you working with one or more partners? Do you have any employees who will be working under you?

Knowing your organizational structure can simplify the process of choosing your legal structure. If you operate your startup alone, a sole proprietorship or single-member LLC structure is likely your best choice. If your startup must include multiple managers and employees from the very beginning, an LLC or corporation structure is probably best.

Legal Structure

The legal business structure you establish will determine how your business is taxed and it will outline your level of personal liability. Many startups and small businesses begin quite simply. Depending on the circumstances of your business, it may expand and be restructured over time, or it can continue to operate in its original form. The most common business structures are sole proprietorships, partnerships, LLCs, and corporations.

A sole proprietorship is ideal for a business that has only one owner and no employees. One of the best features of a sole proprietorship is that in some states you don't need to go through reams of paperwork. It's also relatively easy to file your taxes as a sole proprietor, because your business and personal taxes will be filed on the same return.

As a sole proprietor, you have complete control over the running of your business. One major drawback, however, is that it offers no liability protection whatsoever. In other words, if your business is subject to a lawsuit and you lose, you could potentially lose assets that aren't even related to your business, such as your car or house. If your startup offers a high-risk product or service, you may require a legal structure that provides some personal protection. However, a business with minimal legal risk may benefit, especially in the early days, from organizing as a sole proprietorship.

Another drawback is that banks are often hesitant to offer business loans to sole proprietorships. If you do not yet have a funding source, this business structure may make it more difficult, but not impossible, to obtain funding.

A partnership is a structure in which two or more entities own a business. As with sole proprietorships, general partnerships do not offer full liability protection. In a limited partnership, one partner is a general partner, meaning that he or she still does not have access to liability protection, but the other partners are only held liable for what they've put into the business. In terms of taxes, partnerships file a return that is separate from their personal taxes. This type of tax report basically provides the profits and losses of the business. Although the partnership itself isn't taxed, its profits and losses are passed on to each of its partners. While partnerships are inexpensive to form, they still come with a relatively high share of risk.

Limited liability companies, or **LLCs**, are structures that offer the best form of protection from liability. LLCs are comparable to sole proprietorships because they are easy and relatively inexpensive to set up. It is also possible to file taxes for an LLC on your personal tax return. The main drawback of an LLC is that you may have to pay self-employment tax on your earnings. An LLC is the most common legal structure used by startups.

A **corporation** is a legal structure that separates a business from its owners. Therefore, it offers the most thorough liability protection. The greatest drawback is that a corporation can be relatively expensive to form; it will also more than likely require you to hire a professional accountant to help with its complex form of taxation. The owners of corporations are also doubly taxed on their income.

While you've been learning about the basic business structures, you may find yourself leaning toward one particular form of business. I suggest you consult with a tax accountant, your attorney, and your banker, before moving forward. While you can and probably will restructure your business later, choosing the best initial business structure can have a huge impact on your ability to grow and reach profitability.

After determining your legal structure, you'll need to file all the necessary paperwork and pay the necessary fees to your state government. This is what moves your business from idea to reality. I remember when I officially registered my first business with the state. It was nerve-wracking, but ultimately successful. For the legal structure I originally selected, I was able to file everything online by myself and I was able to print all the documents for later reference. The day that I received my business certificate in the mail, it finally soaked in that I really did officially own a business!

Set Goals and Deadlines

The next step in turning your idea into reality is to start breaking down the overall process of starting your business into individual tasks. One thing that will help you keep moving forward is to set deadlines for accomplishing each task. It's easy to say "I'll get started soon" or "I'll get started eventually," but there are no days of the week called "soon" or "eventually." By breaking the overall process of starting up your business into smaller, more manageable objectives, you're more likely to get it off the ground in good time.

As you read the chapters that follow, you'll be able to detail the activities that need to occur and then assign them appropriate due dates. It is also important to share your goals and deadlines with your team so you all can work together to turn your vision into reality.

Hold Yourself Accountable

When you set goals for completion, it can help to find a way to hold yourself accountable for your actions. Even if you're the most disciplined over-achieving superstar in the world, you'll want to hold yourself accountable for your actions. Launching a startup business is a scary and sometimes overwhelming task, especially for first-time entrepreneurs. This is where an accountability partner can come in handy.

Simply choose a close friend or mentor who really believes in you and your abilities and tell them your specific goals and their due dates. As a due date approaches, your accountability partner will call you up and ask, "Hey, how's your task going?" This way, You'll be forced to say, "It's going great, I've already got it done!" or "I'm working on it but I'm not quite there yet."

This level of accountability can boost your awareness of where you are in your journey to completion. Personally, my skin has been saved many times by my accountability partner. This has happened so many times that I'm now a firm believer in the effectiveness of an accountability structure!

Build and Test a Prototype

Finally, you'll want to create a prototype of your product or a detailed outline of your service. Not only does doing this make your product or service physically real, a prototype also enables you to test its design and functionality. If you have multiple prototypes you can easily compare them. A prototype will also help potential investors determine if your idea is worth the investment of their money.

Most importantly, a prototype enables you to perform user testing before you actually launch your business. User testing can help you improve your product immensely before you make it available to the public. The feedback you receive from the very group of people who will be your future customers can be a huge confidence booster, not to mention that you can use this information to further influence potential backers.

Chapter 4: The Importance of A Business Plan

The development of a business plan is one of the best uses of your time. A business plan lays out a clear definition of your business for potential sponsors, financial supporters, mentors and other allies. It can help keep your business from veering off-course and can help you manage the growth and sustain the profitability of your business over the long haul.

Your business plan is an official document that describes your plan for each major area of your business. It lays out your business goals, your marketing strategies, and your financial plans. For all practical intents and purposes, it *is* your business, especially before daily operations have started up.

A business plan can make it easier to obtain funding through banks or other investors.
Without seeing a completed business plan, nobody will dream of investing money into your business. Potential partners and supporters will expect to see your business plan before they commit to supporting your venture.

As your startup grows, your business plan will change. It remains a living document you adjust as your business shifts to address the realities of the marketplace. You will continue to refer to it as you guide the organization along the path you have outlined for the business. A business plan can make the difference between business success and abject failure.

While some entrepreneurs hire an outside writer to help them craft their business plan, it is actually pretty easy to put together yourself. The description that follows will assist you in this process, giving you a description of each section of your plan.

The Executive Summary

A typical business plan contains nine sections, beginning with the **executive summary**. This summary will make up about ten percent of your entire plan, and will describe, in brief, the contents that follow. Some potential investors *only* read this part, so it is essential that your summary is well-written. You want your readers to see clearly and quickly that you have a great business idea, just waiting to spring to life!

Many entrepreneurs write the executive summary last. After you have wrestled to clearly communicate the details, it will be much easier to pull together a summary that includes the essentials of your business, while they are fresh in your mind. If you prefer to use the summary as a way to outline the key points you intend to write about further on, I recommend you revisit this summary after you're finished. Sometimes things change in the process of providing the details, so you'll want to double-check that your summary still reflects the reality of the rest of your business plan.

An executive summary should introduce your target audience and provide a compelling rationale for the valuable commodity your business intends to offer this audience. At the same time, you will clearly outline *how* your business intends to go about making its products and services available to your target audience.

Most importantly, you must show in your summary how your business will stand out from its competition. You will provide a compelling and realistic three-year financial forecast to demonstrate that your business is worthy of the reader's backing. Finally, it should describe your team and your proposed launch strategy.

Startup Description

Here is where you get to dive into the details of your business. Your startup description should include your business name, the legal structure, the proposed location, and your backstory, including how you came up with the idea in the first place.

This section will also include your **mission statement** and the **vision statement** for your startup. A mission statement briefly describes values of your company and succinctly states the direction your business is headed. Your vision is a brief description how you define success for this venture and the growth you foresee over the first couple years.

Following your mission and vision statements, you should briefly restate your product description summary and repeat the definition of your target audience. Your startup description will close with a list of your **business objectives**. These are essentially the goals you've set for your startup, as a result of performing your industry and market research.

Products and Services

This is where you can provide an in-depth look at what you will be selling. The key is to show how your goods stand out from those sold by your competition. If your selling point is a tangible product, provide an almost photographic-level description of its details. Include a clear portrayal of its physical attributes and special features, while you explain how it will uniquely benefit your target audience. Back up your claims with the results of your market research and describe how you will fulfill your anticipated level of demand, including the resources that will be employed to accomplish this level of production.

Industry Outlook And Market Analysis

You should be familiar with the industry profile from a couple chapters back. You can simply take the information you researched and compile it into a brief report in this section. The main purpose of including this information is to convince potential investors that your startup will be worth their investment. The best strategy is to combine your industry analysis with market research that explores the buying trends of your customers, and add to it your startup's initial budget.

Describing Your Operations

Following your industry outlook and market analysis is the section that is all about your company operations. Startup businesses benefit the most from listing everything they've accomplished so far in terms of operations (e. g., renting an office space or buying supplies). This is one place you'll want to update frequently, as your business really begins to grow and your operations become more complex.

You will want to include here a description of your production process. For example, if you're opening a bakery, you could describe the type and of quantity of resources you'll need in order to produce your line of baked goods, then describe who will be producing them, and how. If you will be operating from a physical location, you will want to describe your storefront hours, your location, and any other information that pertains to your physical operations.

This is also the section to include your quality control methods and to provide the details of your supplier relationships.

Management Team

This section should include information regarding your hiring process and your management breakdown. If you have an advisory board, this is the place to include information regarding the actual and planned makeup of the board.

Setting up an advisory board communicates that you're serious about launching your startup. When you include this in your business plan you communicate that you are willing to take into consideration the wisdom of others as you progress in your business. Advisory board members are often seasoned individuals with first-hand experience in the business world and who can bring specialized knowledge to the table. Your advisory board will meet on a regular basis to discuss important aspects of your business.

Analyzing Your Competition

The competitor analysis is a great way to keep abreast of the market and to show potential investors how you plan to address the competition. Your direct competitors consist of businesses that sell an identical or similar product to yours. An adequate analysis of your direct competitors includes a description of their specific strengths and weaknesses set off against your own, a comparison of the effectiveness of your various locations, an assessment of your target audiences, an evaluation of your individual marketing strategies, an evaluation of your growth outlooks, and a list of any opportunities your competition has missed but you plan to use to your own advantage. It is also helpful to include a SWOT analysis (as described in Chapter 7) in this section of your plan.

Marketing Strategy

The next section is all about how you choose to market your products or services to your target audience in the most efficient way possible. The focus of this plan is to market your product in such as way that you will make a profit without breaking the bank. Marketing can be very expensive, so the right plan will boost sales while protecting your profit margin.

Your marketing plan will describe your market, painting a detailed picture of your ideal client. This is followed by a summary of the marketing analysis you ran on your competition's marketing activities. You then provide an in-depth look at the strategy you plan on using to gain an edge on the competition. Your marketing strategy will include a description of your marketing budget, your strategy to promote and establish your brand, how you plan to employ strategic pricing options, how you intend to effectively distribute your product, and will close with a detailed description of your marketing platform.

Financial Plan

Your financial plan details how you intend to manage your finances, balancing expenses with revenues. It pulls together the various numbers regarding your business in order to show how you intend to guide your fledgling startup through the early days. It details how you plan to balance all the different variables in such a way as to keep financially afloat while you get your product off the ground.

The three essential components of this section are your <u>profit and loss statement</u>, your <u>balance sheet</u>, and your <u>cash flow report</u>. Together, these documents provide a clear picture of the current financial status of your business. Starting with the current status, you can then project where your business will be in six months, twelve months, then two and three years.

Since startups begin with zero live data, your business plan will consist of a sales forecast that shows projected but practical numbers you anticipate your business to generate over the course of the next three years. Of course, you will also explain the rationale behind your projected figures, explaining how you arrived at these numbers.

Much easier to arrive at will be a breakdown of your company's expenses. By detailing your anticipated expenses, you can fairly easily create a realistic business budget, which can help you manage your finances from day one, and plan to offset these expenses with profits.

Writing Your Business Plan

If you are unfamiliar with some of the terminology or strategies I've mentioned here, don't worry; that's what the rest of this book is about. By the time you've worked through the chapters that follow, you'll be prepared to fill in the details of what I've just sketched out. A perfect business plan isn't overly detailed. It just needs to adequately describe your proposed undertaking and be written so as to be understood by the average person.

The Overall Structure

In summary, here are the sections of your business plan. When it comes time to write things out, I suggest you set up a document with each of the following headings, one per page:

- Executive Summary.
- Startup Description.
- Products and Service.
- Industry Outlook and Market Analysis.
- Operations.
- Management Team.
- Competition Analysis.
- Marketing Strategy.
- Financial Plan.

Plan Maintenance

I've stated before that your business plan is a living document. It serves three main purposes. First, it defines the heart and soul of your business, explaining the "why" of its existence and what makes the entity unique. Secondly, it summarizes the current state of your business, reflecting where you are right now. Thirdly, it extends the heart and soul of your business on into the future, quantifying how you envision it will look several years beyond the present.

While the heart and soul of your business may not change, how it is expressed in the real world and how you envision its future will – and should – change as you respond to current market conditions, shifting cultural trends, and an ever-evolving customer base. Correspondingly, your projections into the future will reflect this shift in its starting point.

Review Planning

Because your business will be constantly changing, you will need to adjust its portrait to reflect those changes. The best way to ensure that your plan stays current is to build in – as part of your business plan – a procedure for periodically reviewing and updating it. Reviewing your business plan at least once a quarter can increase the chances that your startup will experience success and see consistent growth.

A business plan helps you structure your business in such a way that it can be easily managed toward success. This makes it easier to obtain funding to support your launch. You can start forming your business plan as soon as you begin to envision your startup. It's okay to start with a sketchy outline and flesh out the details as you go along, but the earlier you get started, the sooner your business dreams can become reality.

Chapter 5: Naming Your Startup

Choosing a name can be one of the fun parts of entrepreneurship. Aside from the fact that the process is creative and exciting, it's another vital factor that can contribute to your venture's success.

Know What You Stand For

What qualities do you want your business to be known for? By this time you should have some idea how to answer this question. Start here. Jot down key terms that describe those qualities, and you'll be well on your way to crafting the perfect name for your business.

Know To Whom You Speak

Revisit your description of your target audience and put yourself in their shoes, asking yourself, "**What motivation is behind my product's attractiveness?**" As you design your company name, keep in mind that it must speak to whatever your target audience hungers for.

These two questions are at the heart of the concept of branding. Furthermore, these truths– what you want to be known for and what your audience is hungry for – will form the core of your marketing efforts. And at the heart of your marketing efforts will be your company name, so it's essential that you embrace a name that supports these values.

Short, Memorable, and Pithy

Ideal business names are often short and easy to remember. The most effective names are often one or two syllables long , three at the very most. For example, consider Uber, Google, and Microsoft, respectively. A long business name that is a mouthful or difficult to pronounce is unattractive and hard to remember. Try thinking of the longest business name you know of – it's hard to find one that is more than three syllables, right?

Avoid coming up with names that are *too* creative, too hard to remember, or lacking any connection with what your business stands for. If possible, pick a short name that is catchy but also reflects the purpose of your products or services. Puns can be clever and easy to remember…if they're not too over the top. But watch out; puns easily sound corny and the pun can actually draw attention away from the character quality you're trying to express, by placing the focus on the pun itself. Yes, it may be memorable, but often for all the wrong reasons.

Domain-Name Friendly

Another important quality of a strong yet unique name is how well it functions as part of the domain name (or website address) you'll be using for your digital presence. Domain names are limited and can be expensive to secure. It's easy to overlook the importance of obtaining an official domain name early in the game. However, if you wait until your presence grows to the point of public recognition, any competitor will have unhindered opportunity to purchase it, potentially taking advantage of your hard-won good name and cutting into your profits. A domain name can be purchased by anyone, so it's better to purchase your ideal domain name early on, before the competition snatches it up.

If the domain name you want isn't available as a dotcom, it is worthwhile to look into other domain extension options, such as ".net" or ".biz." You should also check that you can easily develop a social media presence using the name you settle on. Is there an available Twitter handle, Instagram name, YouTube Channel, Facebook page name or other media availability you expect to build a presence on?

SEO Is Your Friend

The best strategy for picking a name is to pretend like you are optimizing it for a search engine. This can help you enormously when you go to launch an online presence. For example, if your startup will sell top-of-the-line virus protection software, some appropriate keywords would be "anti-virus," "computer protection," and "malware defense." Any online keyword research tool can help you build a list of related keywords. You would then take these keywords and fit them into your business name. For example, "Complete Anti-Virus Computer Protection Software" incorporates a quality descriptive, followed by four relative keywords that potential customers will be highly likely to enter into a search engine. Consequently, when you purchase the domain "completeantivirussoftware.com," your website will likely be one of the first links to pop up and will easily become a memorable name.

There are plenty of domain search tools you can access for free. Just type in your keywords and it will give you a list of matching domains that are available to buy.

Researching Keywords

When you research keywords, don't settle for the first batch you come up with. It is important to find as many keywords as possible and try multiple variations until you come up with something that is strong yet simple, confident, bold, mysterious, and memorable enough to serve as a name for your business. It may help to use a thesaurus to find a variety of synonyms. Even a rhyme dictionary can help you uncover a catchy name that will be what the industry calls "sticky" or memorable.

It is important to avoid words or phrases that have easily confused alternative spellings ("there," "their," and "there" are all similar terms that are commonly mistaken for each other). You'll also want to avoid combining words that don't complement each other. For example, you probably wouldn't use the term "rodents" in the name of a sanitation business unless it is clear that the name reflects the anti-rodent nature of your company.

Names to Avoid

Similarly, avoid business names that just sound bad altogether, names with silent or missing letters in them which will make your name impossible to spell, and avoid names that directly appeal to a limited target audience that may change over time. Avoid trendy names that may not have the same meaning in a few years. Once you have a couple of potential names lined up, check to ensure that the names do not limit your business's growth potential. For example, including the name of your city in your business name may not fare well if your business eventually expands worldwide.

Is It Legal?

You may have already settled on a great business name that communicates strength and confidence but before you get your heart set on it, there are a few things you should find out. First of all, you'll want to check to ensure another person hasn't already trademarked it. You can easily find this out by performing a free search at http://tmsearch.uspto.gov/. You should also run a search within your state. If you choose a business name that is already trademarked by someone else, you expose yourself to various legal risks. The same goes for copyright laws.

Avoid coming up with a name that is painfully similar to giant, existing companies. Avoid parody names like the plague, as they never get very far in the legal world. Starbucks is well-known for jumping on businesses that pop up with even a slight similarity to their name. This is another argument for having a lawyer; your attorney can keep you out of legal trouble by ensuring that you have the rights to the name you have chosen.

Solicit Feedback

Once you have two or three name variations, the next step is to solicit feedback from other people. You can ask your friends and family their opinion, of course, but the most valuable feedback will come from the individuals in your target audience. The best way to test your name against your market is to find a program that will enable you to create and launch multiple web pages using each potential name you've chosen. Then you find a way to direct traffic to each page (via search engine optimization or online ads) and compare the website statistics to see which page generated the most traffic.

Naming Tips

Naming a business requires a combination of art and science. Before you're finished you may feel a little like Goldilocks in her quest for a happy medium! You want a name that is unique but not absurd, descriptive but not too narrow. You want to strike a balance between something that is so comfortable it leaves no impression on the mind and – on the other end of the scale – a name that is so trendy or edgy that it offends or scares away potential customers!

Here are some tips that may help you uncover just the right name for your business:

- Keep it short; two syllables, three if you must. The shorter it is, the harder it is to misspell and the easier it is to glue into your memory.

- Don't use your own name; any negatives associated with your product can easily become associated with your person and taint any future ventures.

- Go back to the first two questions in this chapter and brainstorm descriptive terms that portray those qualities. Use a dictionary, thesaurus, crossword dictionary, or other word-finding aids to help you.

- Avoid terms that connect you to a specific geography or culture; as your business grows, you may well expand your reach beyond your current locale, so avoid boxing yourself in. Allow your vision some space in which to expand.

- Prefer terms nearer the start of the alphabet, closer to "A" than "Z." These terms will show up earlier in searches.

- Avoid puzzle words, obscure references that only a select few would understand (e.g., Norse gods, rare technical terms), acronyms, and obtuse puns. Don't exclude people of average intelligence; instead, pique the curiosity of the regular Joe.

- Seek out ideas primarily from individuals who have something to gain by the success of your business. They have a vested interest that will get you some of the most viable suggestions.

- Stay away from overused prefixes, suffixes, and abbreviations. Avoid mashups involving things like "tron," "tech," "serv," "corp," and the like.

- Avoid purposeful misspellings; they are rarely helpful and often appear trite. The more common misspellings like "nite" and "kwik" do language learners and young readers a disservice, as well as making it harder for people to find you.

Welcoming Improvements

Even after you have settled on what, for you, is the end-all phrasing for your business (or product) name, I advise you to hold it loosely. Times change, trends shift, meaning and usage adjust, and what was once smack-dab in the center of your customers' sweet spot can swiftly find itself totally off the map of their attention.

When they say the only constant is change, they may well have been talking about the world of commerce! Consequently, just as you must regularly review the accuracy of your business plan, you must also set up a process for periodically reviewing the naming and branding of both your business moniker and the names attached to your various products.

Chapter 6: Putting Your Startup on the Map

The location of your operation is a factor that will play hugely in your startup's success! There's more to it than just picking a random empty office or storefront without giving it much attention. Like every other aspect of developing your startup, selecting a location for your business will take thought and research.

General Considerations

When it comes to selecting a location, you'll need to think beyond mere size or attractive appearance. You'll want to consider the location's relevance to your target audience, its proximity to suppliers, ease of access, and where it ranks in relation to the competition. You don't want to be too near – nor too far – from your competition. You'll want to take into account the accessibility of foot traffic, the availability of parking, and the possibility of special event traffic. A startup that develops software for corporate clients would probably do fine with a small office space in an inconspicuous corner of a corporate park, but this would not do at all for a clothing retailer that relies on walk-ins, foot traffic, and impulse sales for its survival. The latter will be looking for an expansive location that is eye-catching, near other retail shops, and easily accessible on foot or by vehicle.

A good location can make or break your startup. It's neither efficient nor practical to just hope you stumble upon a decent, affordable location, especially when your opening is imminent. In this case, you would definitely benefit from a commercial realtor. Less urgent schedules could be accommodated by searches on your local Craigslist, social media "for sale" groups, or through the local chapter of a small business organization.

Many startups rent space in the beginning, since they expect their company to swiftly grow to need something bigger. Of course, you may get lucky and discover the perfect location on your own, but before you jump at the opportunity, please take into account the following considerations.

Accessibility

Where is your target audience located in relation to your physical location? Because a sports bar would tend to attract college students and young adults, it probably wouldn't fare well if it opened up in the midst of an area primarily populated by senior citizens. In the same vein, a senior housing complex would probably not gain many occupants located in the midst of fraternity row near a university campus. Location that is relevant to your customers is highly important, especially now that it's easy to google the closest business of any specific type.

Financial Considerations

A business that requires a storefront should revisit its finances to ensure that it can at least afford an appropriately-sized space to house, display, and introduce its products to potential customers. On the other hand, a service-based operation may require little to no space at all; this is known as a **remote** location.

Certain types of business can benefit from mobile sites, such as food trucks or mall kiosks. Remember, you are not locked into your first location forever – you will be able to move into a larger space as your startup grows. The greatest essential is to choose a location that aligns with the state and federal requirements for your industry, but we'll cover these details in a few pages, so you needn't concern yourself with them right now.

Does It Support Your Brand?

An important factor to consider when choosing your location is how effectively it represents your brand. There are many ways you can reflect your brand through the characteristics of your geography and architecture. For example, some Disney stores have a sparkling bright floor, designed to reflect the childlike wonder the Disney brand evokes in customers of all ages. Many fast food restaurants use a specific interior paint scheme that sends a subliminal message to its patrons to eat their food and get going, thus aligning their physical facility with the concept of "fast" food. Buildings that house the locations for Medieval Times, a business that produces reenactments of medieval tournaments and festivals, are built to look like castles, thus encouraging customers to immerse themselves in the experience of life in the Middle Ages.

How Close Is The Competition

How close is your prospective location to your competition? When I was 16, I worked at a fast food restaurant for a couple of summers. One day, our grill broke down and we were unable to serve burgers, despite the fact that they were our main selling point. That afternoon, a group of guys came in and I told them the bad news about our grill and spelled out our limited menu options. They were deciding what to do when one of friends said, "Hey, there's a cheese steak and pizza place right up the street." I'm sure you can figure out where they ended up having lunch!

Imagine if one day you're unable to provide your customers with what you promise to give them. In the location you're considering, how far would they have to go to get what they're expecting? When your competition is close enough, you'll always risk losing out to them.

However, it is also important to think about it the other way. What if you were the owner of the cheese steak place? You would have just gained a couple of new customers, because your competition was unable to provide them with what they needed. If you provide a unique experience with quality that exceeds the competition, you may actually succeed in winning a customer for life!

When your competition is nearby, it can work out to your advantage, as long as you're prepared. This thought can help motivate you to stay on top of your business and keep your operations running consistently.

Are there any neighboring businesses that might actually help drive sales to your location? This can be another useful strategy. For example, if you're an auto parts shop that opens up down the street from a mechanic shop, it is likely the mechanic who owns the repair shop will become a client of yours, because he will constantly be in need of auto parts.

How Close Are You To Suppliers?

Next, you'll want to consider your location in terms of how close you are to your suppliers. In the example above, the mechanic is very close to a potential supplier, the auto parts shop. I happen to live right around the corner from a produce wholesaler that provides fresh, locally grown produce to local restaurants and grocery stores within a 10-mile radius. It ensures that my neighborhood grocery store is consistently stocked with the freshest of fruits and vegetables!

The benefits of using local suppliers are that it develops strong ties within a community. It also simplifies the matter of finding what you need in a short period of time, allowing you to serve your customers more quickly. I've known restaurant owners to race a nearby grocery store on a rare occasion when they are running low on produce. Proximity to suppliers can make the difference between an ecstatic customer and one who grudgingly waits for a part to arrive, out of sheer necessity.

If the supplies you need are obscure or not locally available, you can pay for the convenience of overnight delivery. In this case, your proximity to major roadways will become a key factor. As you seek out your location, ask yourself what supplies you will require on a regular basis. Then you can pick the best location based partly on how quickly your suppliers can reach you. If you rely primarily on long-haul deliveries, what becomes critically important is how easily drivers can reach your property, especially your loading area. You'll notice that Walmart stores are always located as close as possible to the nearest major highway. They do this purposefully, since almost everything they sell is delivered by semi trailer.

It is also important to consider customers' ease of access to your location. How often have you tried to visit a business, but discovered parking was impossible to find? You probably gave up and headed for a similar business with better parking options.

Businesses that are impossible to locate drive me crazy. One time, I was called for a job interview. I plugged the address into my GPS and drove 40 minutes to the location. However, when I arrived I still didn't know where to go, because there were no signs on the building to indicate an entrance, nor was there an address sign or anything to indicate the name of the business. I ultimately ended up driving away in frustration.

Visibility

What about visibility? Many times I've passed a local business that caught my eye, while on the way to another destination. I would find myself thinking, "That place looks interesting, I definitely want to check it out someday soon!" What caught my eye was not just the location but the fact that I could see the business name clearly.

If you choose to house your business on a busy main street, your visibility may allow you to soak up the benefits of existing traffic. If you choose to house your business on a random street corner, however, you will likely not garner as much drop-in traffic.

If you're in a larger city, don't forget to consider potential customers who do not have a car. Is your location easily accessible by public transportation? Can somebody safely reach your business on a bike? On foot?

The side of the street you're located on can make a significant difference. For example, if most of the traffic on that road flows on the left, your business may not benefit from setting down on the right side of the street. If you own a coffee shop with a drive-through service, you will definitely benefit from situating yourself on the side of the street that gets the most morning traffic!

The Safety Angle

Safety is another important factor in choosing your location, for both your employees and your customers. Don't be afraid to check out the crime statistics for your potential location, and put yourself in the shoes of your customers. Would you want to patronize a business in an area that's unsafe at night? If you're located in a high crime area, you'll probably lose out on evening sales and you'll have a hard time finding employees to work the evening shift. What about an area that's rough at all hours of the day? Would your customers willingly put their safety at risk just to access your products or services?

Soundness Of The Property

Once you've identified a location that appears suitable for your startup, make careful inquires regarding the site's history and its present condition. Image is everything for a business. If you operate out of a building that is falling apart, odds are you won't easily win the trust of many customers. People could fear for their safety and avoid setting foot on your property. At the very least, they would find it hard to trust the quality of what you are offering them. Older buildings tend to require a greater maintenance budget, so you'll want to take that into account. Aging properties are also less likely be prepared to support the electric loads of today's equipment and may not be equipped for newer technology such as Wi-Fi.

Inquiring about the history of the location can save you time and money. You want to approach both renting and ownership with both eyes wide open. If you find out that a location is available because previous businesses did not do well there, you would do well to research why, exactly, they failed. There may also be a reason behind the failures that is unrelated to the businesses themselves.

For example, in my hometown, there was a storefront on the highway that housed an ice cream shop for years. After the ice cream shop moved away, a quick succession of too many businesses to name opened and closed their doors within a five-year period. Why? A rumor had spread around town that the building was infested with termites. Whether true or not, that rumor pretty much rang the death knell for any business brave enough to set up shop in that location.

It's always important learn the history of a building before you sign on the dotted line. This is where a real estate agent can prove invaluable. An agent who knows the area will be able to fill you in on the property's background, including its history of previous owners and tenants.

Legalities To Consider

Don't forget about the legalities of choosing your location. Before settling on a space, you must know that the space is zoned for commercial use. You can easily discover this information by calling the local government offices. Some properties are residential, restricting them for only domestic use. You, however, will be looking for a property in an area zoned for commercial operations. Some areas are also zoned for mixed use, so you won't always be able to guess a property's status, just by looking at its neighbors.

Here's another instance where a real estate agent can be of help; any certified agent should be able to confirm the zoning status of a property. If you are searching properties out for yourself, however, you will want to check with the local government to affirm that you're allowed to do business out of that specific location.

You must also check to see what permits or licenses you will need to obtain before you can open your doors for business. This will call for another visit with local government officials, as well as a query within your industry. For example, a restaurant would most likely require a certificate of approval from a local health inspector. It would also require at least one of its employees to hold food safety certification before it could begin operations. Some businesses, such as salons, also require special permits and have to display certifications of each employee. You will also probably require official approval from a local fire inspector before you can open your business to the public.

As I've already mentioned, you'll need to ensure delivery access to your property. If you are located in a commercial building that happens to neighbor a residential area, chances are, the people living nearby will want assurances that you won't be tearing up their roadways or making noisy deliveries in the middle of the night.

A major convenience store recently opened for business down the street from where I live. Although the property is zoned for commercial use, it is literally next door to a residential street. The residents who lived on that street were understandably concerned about the potential disruption of large trucks bringing in deliveries, the safety of their children playing near those vehicles, and the hassle of large semis blocking the street. After meetings with the neighbors, the business was able to come to an agreement that satisfied the needs of the townspeople. It agreed to only receive deliveries late at night, a solution that effectively answered their concerns.

Since different permits/licenses/certifications are required for different industries, states, and municipalities, I cannot outline their details here. You will need do your own research to learn the details of what you need to accomplish before you can officially open for business.

Help With Pesky Details

Once you've found the perfect location to launch your startup, there are still a few things you'll need to take care of before you sign a rental or purchase agreement. Consider the long-term cost factors of property taxes, utilities, insurance, maintenance, future expansion, and even aesthetic issues such as your paint scheme, furniture, and other aspects of decor. You'll want to be confident that your budget is sufficient for any remodeling that will be necessary before your grand opening.

Yes, this location hunting can be a scary proposition, but don't lose heart. The good news is that your lawyer can usually help you with this process. An attorney is essential to review contracts before you sign them, can assist you in your negotiations for the best lease terms, and can help you deal with your landlord. Most landlords are wonderful to work with, but every once in a while you'll encounter one you'll be quite willing to pass on your attorney!

A commercial realtor can also be a godsend when you're looking for a place to locate your business. A commercial real estate agent will have a vast knowledge of the area and its residents. Commercial realtors will be able to work with you to find an ideal location in light of your property requirements and the customer base you will be serving.

Don't hesitate to gain the services of these professionals. They can be worth their weight in gold. Both can save you from many problems and can steer you away from choices you would deeply regret in the future. Heed their advice. Get a second opinion if you need to, but remember that you are paying them for their experience and their wisdom. Make the most of these two relationships and you won't regret it.

Chapter 7: Your Marketing and Branding Strategy

One of the most important driving factors of success behind your business will be your customers, so ensuring you're in direct and constant communication with your target audience is crucial for driving sales. After all, without customers you have no sales and with no sales you have no business.

Instead of marketing to everybody in hopes of generate sales to a few, you can benefit greatly from marketing to a specific group of people who are highly likely to buy from you. This specific group of people is known as your target audience.

Identifying the demographics of your target audience can be simple to figure out, but more often than not, it will require time, experimentation, and effort. Your target audience may in reality be different than you planned for, so you may need to quickly adjust the focus of your marketing. However, knowing your target audience makes it possible for you to directly market your product to prospective customers who will be the most likely to respond favorably to your efforts.

Market Your Expertise

As a startup entrepreneur, your goal is to develop a relationship with your target audience. The best way to gain their business is to first figure out exactly who that audience is, to discover what is their greatest problem, and offer your product as a solution. I once knew a lawyer who specialized in the area of drug law. He had a huge presence on an online message board where people who were facing misdemeanor drug charges could freely ask questions about what to expect in court, and whether they had a chance to fight the charges against them.

The lawyer would provide basic answers to those questions, using examples from his previous successful cases. This positioned him both as an expert and a caring individual. Although he was passionate about the enforcement of laws regarding drugs and drug use, his listening ear and kind, truthful responses made him look like an expert people could trust. As a result, almost everyone who talked to him wanted him to represent them in court. He even had prospective clients asking how far he was willing to travel to represent them! All of this success came from marketing himself through a free service that placed him in the center of a community that valued his expertise.

Problem-Solving For Your Target Audience

Your target audience has a problem you're determined to solve, a need you're resolved to address. It must be narrowed down to a very specific niche that leaves no gaps or unanswered questions. The worst way to define your target audience is to identify it as everyone. Even identifying your target audience as stay-at-home dads, elementary school children, or dog owners isn't specific enough. A more specific example would be "male dog owners with an annual income of $100,000 who live in New York City." You could even narrow it down further to "single African American beagle owners with an annual income of $100,000 who live in New York City." Include as many specific details as possible.

After you have identified a potential target audience you have to make sure it is a large enough group to be profitable. You don't want to narrow your audience down to the point that you only have a handful of possible consumers. If you find your audience is too narrow, go back and retune it to see if you can access a broader range of people without becoming too generic.

What Are You Really Selling?

If you're unsure where to begin, go back to your product descriptions and break them down into specific benefits. One great trick I learned is to figure out what you're *really* selling; that will narrow down your target audience quite easily. This is also known as identifying your **Unique Selling Proposition** or USP.

For example, a cosmetic company may technically be selling makeup products, but in essence it's selling beauty. A 24/7 corner store may technically be selling beverages, snacks and magazines, but what it's really selling is convenience. Take a look at your product or service and look for the essence of what you're selling. Then think about who is most drawn to this essence. For example, the cosmetic company that is selling beauty will likely appeal to high school girls who are highly body aware and trying to appear more mature or to adults who may be trying to appear younger than they feel. The corner store that sells convenience will likely appeal to travelers passing through town or busy parents stopping in on their way home from work. When you narrow down your business to what you're really selling, it can make the process of identifying your ideal client much simpler.

If you're still stuck, you may discover some answers by looking at your competition. Begin by seeing if you can pinpoint *their* target audience. Of course, their audience may not match yours perfectly; you want it that way. Otherwise you would have a much greater challenge addressing the competition. However, if you can identify your closest competitor's target audience, you'll be well on your way to identifying your own.

Your Ideal Client Profile

Your ideal client profile is a snapshot of what your perfect client looks like, give or take a few details. Once you have written down this description it will become a key part of your business plan and will determine the tone and focus of your marketing efforts.

When developing your ideal client profile, you should consider demographic factors such as age, gender, race, religion, ethnicity, education level, income level, family size, marital status, personality, interests, values, and anything else that is important to your marketing strategy. You may not specify every one of these details, but it is important to hone in on those specifics that make this the perfect candidate for your product or service.

When you are open for business, you will actually begin to pick up patterns among your clients that can help you further hone in on the details of your ideal client. As you modify your ideal client profile you will be able to tweak your marketing efforts to more effectively reach these clients.

Market To Their Motivations

When you know what to look for in an ideal client you can start to investigate his or her motivations and use that to your advantage in your marketing strategy. When you know the values of your client base, you can use those values to effectively speak to the emotions of your audience.

If you've ever seen children's food items advertised on TV as "healthy" and "parent-approved," then you know what it is like to market to customers based on values. The marketers know that most parents want to be perceived as great parents, not only by themselves but also by their peers and their own children, so they are more likely to provide their children with food that is perceived as "healthy." because society knows that good health is paramount. Marketers know this; they know that if they market a food item as healthy, it will align with the values of their target audience.

Some other values that are commonly addressed by corporate advertising include ego, self-esteem, health, family, relationships, and sex. The next time you watch television, try to identify which of these themes are addressed by the advertising that pops up.

Serve Your Customers

You should know your target audience inside-out. You should know where they gather, both online and in the real world. You should know how they like to obtain their information, whether they read newspaper or magazine articles, watch television, stream news online, or listen to the radio. With enough market research, you can glean almost any details you want about your target audience. Armed with this information, you are now able to design your marketing plan to speak effectively to your specific target audience.

At the same time you are devising a marketing plan, you are also involved in building relationships. Nobody likes to be sold to. Rather, they want to know that you are a real person, connecting to them on the basis of your mutual humanity. If you head into your marketing activities with this thought in mind, you will be able to effectively connect with your audience on a personal level. There are many ways you can communicate effectively. In addition to the traditional snail mail promotions and physical coupons, you can stay in touch with your audience by sending out the occasional survey, carefully scheduling a series of email messages, or via any number of social media platforms.

In addition to blatant sales promotions, your customer base will also respond well to what I call "supportive services." Blogs are very useful for this purpose, as are social media posts. Supportive services are free offerings (at least free to the consumer) that are related to the theme of what you are selling.

With these offerings, you further address the root needs that you have already determined are part of the makeup of your target audience. If you provide a cosmetic that promotes healthy skin, an article that shows how specific foods can benefit the skin will answer a genuine need of this population. In this article you are aligning your company with that deep-seated need, as a solution provider. You are also communicating that you care about the customer. This is all the more powerful because the customer can access this information for free. You are communicating that your goodwill extends beyond what you can get out of it.

It can also go a long ways toward winning their loyalty when you reach out to your customers for no profit-related reason. A business that reaches out periodically just to say "Thanks for your business," is much more likely to be remembered and respected by its target audience than other organizations that rely on a reputation based solely on point-of-sale interactions.

Your Marketing Strategy

Your marketing strategy is how you plan to spend your marketing budget, hopefully in the most effective way possible. A strong marketing strategy outlines your marketing goals and reflects the message you want to send to your audience. Once you have a marketing strategy mapped out, you can begin to develop your **marketing plan**, where you outline how you will implement your marketing strategy.

Marketing Strategy Design

A **marketing strategy** outlines where you intend to focus your marketing. Your **marketing plan** describes how you will apply this strategy to your marketing budget.

Knowing the motivations of your audience is a good way to start creating a marketing strategy. For example, if your product aligns with the need of your ideal customer to provide their family with a healthy snack option, your marketing strategy should focus on communicating the benefits of healthy eating. The trick is to determine the values or needs of your particular audience and brainstorm a list of as many possible benefits related to the need your product or service addresses.

The second step is to figure out how you can come up with a more efficient marketing strategy than your competition, so you're getting the most value out of your own marketing budget. If your competition focuses primarily on the healthy qualities of the snack they're producing, perhaps you can emphasize the sustained energy your product provides. With a solid competition analysis and accurate market research, it should be fairly simple and straightforward to develop your customized marketing strategy. Since trends and demand are constantly shifting, you will want to establish a practice of revisiting your marketing strategy every few months, to keep yourself in the center of your audience's attention.

Developing A Marketing Budget

The next step is to create a budget that fits with your marketing needs. Creating a budget for anything can be an overwhelming task so I will break it down in a way that makes it easy to understand.

The first question you'll want to ask of yourself and your business is, "**How much** of my profits should I allocate toward marketing?" In the marketing industry, the general rule of thumb is to allocate up to 10% of the profits you make. New startups can increase that percentage and spend a little bit more in order to grab the attention of their target audience with their new product. Startups and established businesses alike should also look into how much their competitors are allocating toward marketing. All in all, the key is to be realistic and practical, as is the case with creating any type of budget. Don't pour all of your profits into marketing, but at the same time, don't under-spend and fail to adequately represent your business.

The second step is to figure out the **methods** of marketing you plan to use. Although some methods can be pricey, the good news is that the best methods for our times (i.e. digital marketing methods) are often highly effective and good for your business's wallet. A good rule of thumb is that as long as you can provide your audience with high quality marketing content, it doesn't really matter how much money you spend on marketing.

Marketing Plan Design

Your marketing plan shows *how* you will put your marketing strategy into action. For example, if the majority of your target audience does not use social media, then it would be pointless to spend money on Facebook ads or on film-editing software for YouTube videos. Yet, with proper analysis, you should be able to determine where to best invest your marketing dollars. The process begins with an analysis of your strengths and weaknesses.

SWOT Analysis

The first step is to perform a **SWOT analysis** of your business and your competition. The SWOT acronym stands for strengths, weaknesses, opportunities, and threats. This analysis can be a powerful tool. It provides a visual summary of four characteristics of your business that have the greatest influence on your potential for success. A SWOT analysis can help you identify great marketing opportunities that will enable you to exceed your competition.

The first step of the SWOT analysis is to draw a simple four-square grid The top two squares make up the internal factors; the bottom squares represent the external influences. The internal factors are the strengths and weaknesses associated with your business. The bottom two squares represent two types of external factors that affect your business. The bottom left square is where you will list the positive opportunities that your business can walk through to increase its success. The bottom right square will contain all the potential threats to any aspect of your business, all the external factors that would work against your success.

Once you've created a SWOT analysis for your business, you'll want to complete a similar analysis for your closest competitor. Then you can compare the two, side by side, to identify any marketing opportunities you may have to your advantage.

The Four Ps

After performing your SWOT Analysis, the next step is to develop and utilize the four Ps of marketing. This analysis tool was developed by marketing professor, E. Jerome McCarthy, and has proved an invaluable resource for numerous businesses since its inception. The four Ps summarize the primary aspects that impact any marketing effort.

Product

The first "P" stands for "product." The product design or product packaging can be used as a powerful marketing leverage (e. g., recyclable packaging or easy to open packaging). Other factors to consider for marketing leverage are product warranties, return policies, and quality levels.

Pricing

Part of the value of your product how good your price appears, in comparison with the benefits it offers. Slapping an arbitrary price on your product belies the fact that pricing has an impact on more than just the profitability of your business. Your pricing influences the customer's perception of product quality and it factors into whether they view your product as a good deal, or simply "cheap." Consequently, your pricing strategy must take into account the results of extensive market research.

Many people love to purchase inexpensive food because they tend to go through it quickly. However, other consumers are willing to pay a higher price for something that will add healthy nutrients and avoid contributing toxins to their environment. In short, they are willing to pay more for something that will truly bring them added value. A person looking for a new car is often willing to pay more for something new, full of features, and with a high safety rating. Likewise, professionals are often willing to pay more for high quality services that can catapult their business forward.

Don't forget that you also have the option of offering discounts, promotional pricing, and payment plans to add attractiveness to your offerings. These, too, are part of the pricing aspect of marketing.

Promotion

Promotion focuses on boosting the attractiveness of your products or services to your target audience through public relations, general advertising, or targeted sales. For example, authors who self-publish on Amazon have the option of offering their books at a free or highly discounted promotional price every couple of months. The purpose is to increase awareness of the author in hopes of driving future sales.

Placement

Placement is also known as **distribution.** Physical placement refers to the specific locations where your customers can get their hands on your goods. The placement of a special hamburger might be a fast food restaurant. The placement of a book might be a bookstore or an online retailer. The placement of a pest service could be a website where you can offer consultations, or it might be the small sign strategically placed outside the home of a happy customer.

The way you distribute your goods is important because any lack of accessibility will limit your sales. The primary question you need to answer is, "How will my customers buy my product?" Will they buy directly from your business, through a sales team? Will they buy your feline product at major pet stores? Will your products be available for purchase online? If so, what online platforms will you use?

Marketing Methods

Here are some of the most popular marketing methods in use today:

- *Paper Stuff:* The benefit of flyers, handouts, or posters is that they cost-effective; you can usually get a bulk printing discount for large quantities. Another benefit is that you can sometimes include a cut-out coupon on your flyers or handouts to motivate customers to try your business.

- *Sidewalk Chalk Art:* Although this is not a traditional method of marketing, it can be helpful if your business is located in an area with lots of foot traffic. All you'll need is a piece of chalk, a dry day, and a section of sidewalk you can use to communicate your message and promote your business.

- ***Snail Mail:*** Although email dominates snail mail, some businesses may benefit from sending "freebies" such as physical coupons or free samples to their customers

- ***Telemarketing:*** Telemarketing is a marketing method by which a salesperson sells a product or service to a customer over the phone. Although telemarketing tends have a negative reputation, especially with the rise of telemarketing scam calls you've probably received, some startups may be able to use it in an effective manner. Instead of trying to sell something outright, you or a member of your team could call customers to simply inform them about a new promotion you're offering. You could also call just to "check in" and let your customers know you're thinking of them. Doing so tends to create rapport, which can contribute to developing good customer relationships, which can bring the customer to your door, you get the picture.

- ***Email Marketing:*** Email marketing is a method by which businesses communicate with their customers via email. Businesses often offer coupons, promotions, deals, or newsletters through email marketing. This is a great way to develop brand recognition across your target audience. One of the best benefits of email marketing is that many programs are available that give you real-time statistics on who opens your messages, how many times they are viewed, etc. These statistics provide valuable feedback on the efficiency of your marketing, allowing you to tweak your messages and your audience to develop an excellent email marketing plan. This form of marketing is highly cost efficient and does not pollute the environment with unwanted paper. The potential disadvantage is that many email platforms filter out emails from businesses as "spam" and the emails can get lost in customers' reject files.

- ***Social Media Marketing:*** Social media offers one of the best marketing opportunities available to startups. This type of marketing utilizes platforms such as Facebook, Twitter, and Instagram to reach an intended audience. Facebook alone has nearly two billion users, affording businesses the ability to reach a huge proportion of their target audience for relatively little cost.

- ***Print Ads:*** Print ads include advertisements that are run in periodicals such as magazines, catalogs, yellow pages, and newspapers. This type of marketing leans more toward advertising, which is a marketing method that doesn't focus on a target audience but seeds an entire area in hopes of reaching customers.

- ***Blogging:*** Blogging is a popular method of giving out free information. It's also great for attracting potential customers through search engine optimization. Most website hosts enable users to include a built-in blog on their website for easy access by visitors.

Putting It All Together

Now that you have all the pieces, it's time to put them all together into your finished plan. A complete marketing plan should include:

- A brief description of the marketing challenges you face.

- An overview of your four Ps.

- A SWOT analysis.

- A summary of the marketing methods you intend to use to communicate with your target audience.

Your Brand Strategy

Your brand strategy differs from your marketing strategy in that your brand isn't about your products or services or even your business name or logo. Your business brand is similar to your trademark in that <u>it identifies your products and services as coming from your particular business.</u> A brand is the essence of what differentiates your product from its generic version.

The ways in which you choose to place your brand before other people is your brand strategy. In addition to linking your brand to your products, you will use it as leverage in your marketing strategy, to persuade consumers to purchase from your business rather than from your competition. For example, Bounty has branded its paper towels as strong and reliable. When customers are shopping for paper products, they are more likely to perceive Bounty paper towels as the stronger of the choices. The power of the brand influences sales.

In this chapter, you will also discover how to create an effective branding strategy to mark your products and services as desirable. It's your branding strategy that will create positive, long-lasting impressions and will attract buyers.

Analyzing Your Marketing Effectiveness

Last but not least, you'll want to be able to analyze the results of your marketing efforts to see if your marketing strategy/plan is working. For example, you may be spending the majority of your marketing budget on email marketing but you actually might not be getting a great response. If that's the case, why continue to spend your money on email? Marketing analysis can also help you figure out exactly how much it is costing you to gain a new customer and to maintain your relationship with existing customers. Startups may not initially get the results they want, but as long as they analyze the results of their marketing strategies, they eventually will be able to learn what will work.

Most marketing tools include analysis features. Have you ever visited a website or a business and been asked the question, "How did you hear about us?" This is one way you can track your marketing effectiveness. By asking this simple question, you can discover the primary way potential customers are reaching you. Once you have this information, you can focus on putting more money into the methods that most effectively gain you new customers.

No two startups are the same. No two marketing plans are ever the same, either. Radio and TV ads may work wonders for one business, but another might be better served by focusing its marketing efforts on social media websites.

Branding Strategy

Branding is the part of a marketing strategy in which a business employs a specific name, picture, label, or slogan to make its products or services stand out from the crowd of similar products. Branding was originally used by cattle drivers; it consisted of burning an identifying mark on the flank of the cattle they owned. Today, branding has extended its reach into the business world as a way to identify your products and differentiate them from all the similar offerings out there.

The purpose of business branding is to leave your target audience with a specific impression about the nature of your product or service. For example, Bounty paper towels leaves its customers with the impression that they are the best paper towels available on the market. They are known as being strong, durable, and good for cleaning up a mess. The Tide brand leaves the impression that it's the best laundry detergent for fighting stains and getting your clothes clean without damaging your fabrics.

Brand Loyalty And Brand Equity

We use branding to generate **brand loyalty**. Once a person uses a product or service and experiences the quality behind a specific brand, he or she is most likely to continue using that brand. Employees who are loyal to your company are more likely to continue working for it. Customers who like the distinctive flavor of your new soda will prefer it over all others. When individuals are confident that your brand consistently represents a specific quality they value or appreciate, you will have built brand loyalty

Brand loyalty can extend to what is known as **brand equity.** Customers who have positive experiences with one product are likely to extend that positive vibe to other products produced by your company. Once this generalizing of loyalty occurs, customers will be willing to spend more money in order to get their hands on products with your brand on them. When you've achieved brand equity, it greatly increases the overall value of your business.

All in all, the purpose of branding is to communicate the benefits of a product or service to a customer on an internal, subconscious level, to the point that the customer associates specific emotions with your brand and actually experiences those emotions when engaging with that brand. This brand association connects the product to a pleasant sensory memory: an aroma, a color, a taste, a unique delightful texture or a refreshing auditory experience.

Review Customer Benefits

Think back for a moment to your unique selling proposition (USP). Remember, your USP is what makes your goods or services unique from similar offerings. You can use this to gain leverage as part of your brand strategy; it will provide the main driving point behind all your marketing plans.

With your USP in mind, draw up a list that contains every single benefit a potential customer within your target audience may conceivably experience from using your product or service. Once you have created your list, your next step is to identify the benefits you believe will have the greatest positive impact on sales. Identify the words that are most likely to get stuck in your customers' heads. Look for words that evoke specific emotions, phrases that pique their curiosity or resonate with their specific place in life.

Align With Customer Values

Think back to earlier in this chapter where we discussed common customer values, such as health and ego. Consumers are more likely to want to use products and services from a company when those products or services align with their values. For example, when I was 13 years old, I briefly got into the punk music and skateboarding scenes; I wanted to feel like a skater and be viewed by others as a punk rocker. For that period of time, I only wore Vans sneakers and accessories. Vans had a huge reputation as a skateboarding shoe and it sponsored popular music festivals.

Think of the makers of Old Spice deodorant; they market its message of "smelling like a man," to men who want to feel masculine. How can your product similarly align itself with the longings of members of your target audience? Use that quality to your advantage! Once you have identified what your company stands for, what are the most evocative qualities of your brand, and how your customers want to identify with it, you can begin to use these elements to mold the way people view your brand.

Setting Brand Objectives

The two main questions to ask when establishing your brand objectives are:

- How do I want my brand to affect my business in terms of growth, sales, and reputation?

- How do I want people outside of my business to perceive my products or services?

Use these questions as a springboard for noting ideas that describe specific objectives for your company and your brand. Cluster similar ideas together, then take each idea clump and work those words around until you have come up with one or two short sentences that clearly portray each unique objective you want to reach with your brand.

Set Goals To Support Your Marketing Objectives

Objectives describe *what* you intend to accomplish with your business. The next step is to figure out *how* you plan to get to that spot. For this, you will need to set up some goals.

Goals are the place where your objectives take on flesh. Your goals define the spot where your dreams intersect with reality. As such, you must stop thinking in generalities and start thinking in specifics that can be evaluated. For, if you cannot clearly objectify a goal, how will you know whether you've reached it or if you have farther yet to go?

Set In Time

Each goal you set must possess three qualities. First it must be **time-bound**. Your goal must have some sort of time by which you expect to have it completed. There is a universal law that states all tasks will expand to fill the amount of time allotted to them. According to this statement, known as Parkinson's law, if you give a task two months, it'll take all of two months to accomplish. However, if you set the deadline at two weeks, amazingly enough, most of the time you'll be able to finish the necessary work easily within that time frame. If you crunch down the time it'll require to the shortest amount possible, you'll reach your goals in record time. On the other hand, we've all had those things we intend to get around to doing "someday." They never get done, largely because there's no fence around the task, no ending time boundary.

Quantifiable

The second requirement of any goal is that its endpoint be measureable. If your objective is to establish sustainable profits and you want to set up goals in support of that objective, you'll need to first define precisely what you mean by "sustainable profits." In this case, you will be looking for a dollar figure, something specific that you can measure your work against.

Once you have that dollar figure, you can break the final amount into stages and plan out specifically what you intend to do to reach each of these benchmarks. When you first start out, you may find it hard to pin yourself down to a specific goal amount. It's no problem if your initial measureable quantity is incorrect, so don't waste time worrying over it. The amount can always be adjusted to better reflect the demands of the marketplace. Then, as you gain experience, you will be better able to estimate what it will take to convert your objectives into measureable goals.

Achievable

The purpose of setting goals is to stretch you, but not to defeat you. The idea is to enhance your skills and abilities, not to destroy yourself in the process. Consequently, it's essential that any goal you set out to accomplish is actually doable, given your present resources and capabilities. This guideline helps you to set yourself up for success.

If you review a goal and find it impossible to reach with your existing skills, abilities, and resources, then it's time to back up a step. If your goal is a valid one, you'll want to evaluate what you need if you're going to step out after it. Set an intermediate goal that will take you closer to having what you need to reach what you are really after. Once that goal is reached, you can re-establish your original goal.

For each goal you come up with, you'll want to devise an action plan. How will you achieve that goal? For example, if one of your goals is to grow your customer base by 40% over the course of six months, the action you may choose is to increase brand awareness by implementing specific marketing strategies you outline in your action plan.

If your objective is to become the most trusted brand of dish soap by the end of the year, a goal could be to develop a formula that will leave dishes squeaky clean. Your action plan would consist of research and repeated experimentation until you come up with a formula that meets your specific quality criteria.

Multiple Branding

It is possible to have multiple brands within your brand, which can be another aspect of your branding strategy if applicable. For example, Kellogg is a huge, well-known brand for manufacturing ready-to-eat snacks and breakfast foods. Kellogg also owns the brands Keebler, Eggo, and Morningstar Farms. The benefits to bundling multiple brands under your primary brand are that it supports flexible marketing/USPs, product variety, and in a way it also serves as an "insurance policy" for your main brand.

Kellogg's brand, Keebler, is marketed as a snack to children and Eggo is marketed as a healthy breakfast option for children and parents. Each product has its own benefits that appeal to a distinct section of Kellogg's overall target audience. Since Kellogg targets both adults and children, having multiple brands of products enables the company to do this easily. Finally, if the Keebler brand was to ever fail horribly, Kellogg could still stand on the strength of its other brands.

The drawback of multiple branding is that it can split your target market, complicating your marketing efforts. You can actually steal sales from yourself if you're not careful. The costs of marketing multiple brands to multiple populations can grow exponentially. When you're first starting up, I recommend you limit yourself to a single brand, just to keep matters simple. As your company grows, you'll be able to grow your brands and develop your marketing to keep pace with these expansions.

Revisit And Tweak

Once you have set a marketing plan in place, you will want to review it every year, possibly monthly in the early days of your startup. Because your target audience consists of humans, you'll want to review your marketing plan frequently to ensure your message is still current. Humans are constantly changing, influenced by trends, technology booms, and busts, and other variable factors in the economic environment, so your marketing plan will need to be revised frequently to stay on top of these changes.

More than likely, you will be able to make small tweaks to keep your message in line with the needs of your audience. Periodically, however, circumstances will have shifted so massively as to require a complete overhaul of your marketing strategies.

Remember, there is a difference between successful brands and brands that will not survive for long. Successful brands not only align with their customers' beliefs but they also have established a relationship with their customers. They interact on a regular basis. This is easier now than ever, thanks to the availability of social media platforms.

Successful brands are consistent. Their target audience knows what to expect. Unsuccessful brands often change their strategy when the company is hurting without keeping their target audience in mind.

Successful brands only change strategies when it is necessary to align with the changing attitudes and values of their target audience. As with your marketing strategy, use your brands in alignment with the marketing channels that are most successful for your business to drive the most sales, boost brand awareness, and increase brand loyalty. The key to developing a great brand is to truly stand out with something that is uniquely memorable. Customers are more likely to remember you when you do something different from the run of the mill stuff your competitors are doing.

Business Development Strategy

After these are established, you'll find it helpful to develop a great **business development strategy**. Business development is when you expand your customer-base in order to increase sales. In many cases, the business development branch of a company is so large that they have a designated person in charge of overseeing the development of sales. A business development strategy combines sales, marketing, and analysis to help a business determine how and when to expand its target audience.

Business development is a complex field, involving a great deal of planning, promotion, and the application of multiple short- and long-term goals. Startups can especially benefit from business development because they start out small but their success depends largely upon their growth. Startups can survive without a business development strategy in the beginning, but this will be essential for the ongoing life of the business.

There are several important questions you should ask of your business when the time comes to begin planning business development:

- Where does the business currently stand? Where should it stand in the next year, three years, five years, etc.?

- What do we need to do differently to achieve our development goals?

- What obstacles or roadblocks stand in the way of reaching our development goals?

- What will be the results of reaching our development goals?

Next, you can begin focusing on the actual process of acquiring new customers. Did you know that acquiring a new customer can cost a startup 15 times the resources it takes to maintain a positive relationship with an existing customer? Don't panic at that statistic. The good news is that much of your new business can grow out of your existing business. There are often many untapped opportunities hiding out within your existing target audience, just waiting for you to take advantage of them.

Aside from continued business, it is important to consider a theory similar to the snowball effect. This rule suggests that for every customer you have, that customer has at least 50 friends, family members, and acquaintances. Any of those 50 or so people have the potential to become new customers, thanks to word-of-mouth, referrals, or direct communication.

Now that you've figured out what you stand for and have developed clear strategies for reaching your target audience, let's turn our attention to the people who will make your strategies possible, your startup team.

Chapter 8: Building Your Startup Team

At the beginning phase of many startups, the founders typically run the business themselves. However, as a startup gains popularity and you start to taste success, you will see the need to bring on additional employees who can run day-to-day operations while you steer the organization to even greater success. If you fail to develop a team when your business reaches this stage, you may well wear yourself out with all the effort it takes to both run the business and manage its growth. To avoid business burnout, this chapter will help you build the ultimate operations management team. With the right people at your side, you can continue to run your business happily and successfully.

Letting Go

If you're really stubborn like I am, you'll probably face some internal resistance when it comes to putting together a team. It can be nerve-wracking to set others in charge of key business elements, but the right people can make your job much easier. As humans, we all have our strengths and weaknesses, our talents and skills. There is no such thing as a person who can do everything. For example, you may be an extremely talented writer but a terrible graphic artist. This means you'll need to add to your team an employee who *is* a skilled graphic artist to help you design the cover illustrations for your books.

You may be the best singer in the world, but you'll need someone to promote your music. The great news about developing a business team is that it comes with many benefits. In addition to increasing the strength and diversity of your capabilities by hiring individuals to shore up your weaknesses and address specific needs, you are adding intelligence and breadth of problem-solving capacity to your business. Building a great team can also help with networking and relationship-building.

Structuring Your Business Team

Let's begin by learning about the primary positions typically included in any large corporation. Startups generally do not need to fill these positions immediately, but the functions they perform will be evident in embryonic form from the very beginning. Your awareness of what these positions contribute to your operation will help you envision what your business can look like when it is fully fleshed out.

The officer positions that appear in most major corporations are:

- Chief Executive Officer (CEO)

- Chief Operating Officer (COO) or President

- Chief Financial Officer (CFO)

- Chief Marketing Officer (CMO)

- Chief Technology Officer (CTO)

Come along with me as we unpack each of these offices.

CEO stands for Chief Executive Officer. The person who holds this position is commonly the "top dog" of the company. The CEO oversees and decides things such as the company mission and vision, the development of the management team, where most of the money goes, and similar factors. Most of the CEO's power centers around establishing, developing, and managing the rest of the management team. All in all, the CEO is the person responsible for steering the company's ship safely through the dangerous waters of the competitive business world.

COO stands for Chief Operating Officer and can sometimes be combined with the office of President. As the title states, this position focuses on the operations portion of the business. The main responsibility of this individual is to monitor the running of company operations and to ensure that they are cost-effective and representative of the company's values. The duties of a president may also be included, along with aspects of financial oversight. While the details of this office can vary widely, this is the general description.

CFO stands for Chief Financial Officer. A CFO is the main person responsible for handling the financial side of the business. A CFO commonly manages your budget and develops a spending strategy, selecting the best purchasing options available. This office calls the shots on which products or services are worth keeping or developing further, and which need to be revamped, remarketed, or dropped because they are a financial drain. This officer will keep one finger on the pulse of the target audience and an eye out for shifts in popular trends. A CFO can remove much of the burden of financial responsibility, from your shoulders. Unless you are a financial wizard yourself – and even if you are – you will benefit by bring on board an individual you can trust to responsibly steward your finances.

CMO stands for Chief Marketing Officer. The CMO is the person responsible for overseeing your company's marketing and sales strategy. This individual is responsible for understanding your particular industry as well as your target audience, your unique selling proposition (USP), your competition, and anything else that is part of your marketing. This position has emerged quite recently on the corporate landscape. You may not need to institute a separate marketing office until this part of your business has grown too complex and unwieldy to manage by yourself.

CTO stands for Chief Technology Officer; it is also a relatively recent arrival to the corporate structure. However, with technology playing an increasingly important role in multiple aspects of any business, it is worth considering. The main responsibility of a CTO is to research and stay ahead of trends in technology while keeping the organization's computer systems running effectively and efficiently.

Which Offices Do You Need?

A startup probably won't need to fill these offices in its beginning stages. In fact, the best way to decide which positions you need and which you can do without is to take a realistic assessment. Let's pretend you are creating a startup in the form of a partnership. You have a marketing background while your partner has solid financial management training and experience. Although you someday will need to hire employees to oversee the financial and marketing aspects of your business, it would make the most sense for you and your partner to oversee these parts of the startup, thus saving plenty of money while not jeopardizing your business. You and your partner will be able to focus somewhat on the part of the business you each do best; you can defer to your partner's expertise, freeing yourself from stress and worry in the areas in which you are weakest.

However, let's say neither of you are any good with the financial end of your business. While you could rely heavily upon an external accountant in the beginning, you would soon need to find a competent and trustworthy financial officer.

With a small team of three founders, your startup probably won't need an operations officer, but as it proves successful you would be wise to add the position; it will help keep your company afloat. Once you've converted to a corporation, you can shift away from your focus on marketing and sales to take on the CEO position. At that point, you would need to fill the gap with a skilled marketing officer (CMO).

Your business is in no way constrained to the five positions I have described above. Your needs will vary, depending on your type of business, and what you deem necessary to establishing your success. While you'll eventually need officers in charge of sales and marketing, finances, and technology, you may also need SEO experts, computer programmers, content writers or any number of other skilled individuals.

As you are developing your business structure, early on you will want to brainstorm a list of each essential function that will have to be performed in order to implement your business. While you may not need to hire five content writers in the beginning phases, you will need at least one person who can fill that function from day one. In the beginning, one person may well fill multiple functions but as the business develops, you will probably need to add individuals to share the responsibilities.

Without these essential functions your business just won't run. It's like trying to start your car when your gas tank is empty and your battery is dead.

Expanding Your Team

In the end, most startups begin with a small team and add positions as needed. It is helpful to start out small because you'll be paying out a salary to each team member. The advantage of startups is that many team members will be willing to settle for lower salaries in the beginning, understanding that as the business succeeds and grows, their salary will grow along with it. One way you can encourage this mindset is to promise your employees a percentage of sales as part of their pay. That way, you're still able to make a profit but you'll be able to pay your employees a fair percentage of what your company is worth.

As business increases, you will be able to afford to pay more and higher salaries. A good way to avoid stretching your budget with large salary outlays in the beginning is to avoid hiring full-time employees. A part-time finance manager or a part-time marketing manager may well be all you need at first.

You may also want to explore the option of hiring independent contractors. Contractors can be brought in to serve a specific phase of your business development, to complete a specific project, or on an as-needed basis. You may be able to pay them on a lower hourly basis than you would pay a full-fledged corporate officer. Just vet your contract workers carefully to ensure you get the right skill sets for your business needs.

Tips for Building Startup Teams

- Stick to bringing on people you've worked with before or at least ensure that you are familiar with their skills. This will help everything to run smoothly during the early phases of your startup. The last thing you want is to do the setup work incorrectly, only to discover that things don't work right when you launch your business and you have to correct mistakes in the middle of running it.

  When you bring on people whose work you haven't yet seen, you take on the risk of their work and their skills not being up to par. Avoid using classified ads or internet job boards for posting openings for executive positions. For these roles I recommend working with professional networking, professional social media platforms such as LinkedIn, or through professional job search services. Networking opportunities can also help you target the type of individuals with the skills you need. For example, you just might find your new marketing manager by attending a marketing seminar and interacting with the participants and leaders.

- Surround yourself with a team that has diverse and varied experience. Look for people with a solid track record of success. If they have experience with startups, all the better. Of course, that doesn't mean you should automatically skip over people with a promising resume who lack experience. Sometimes it's easier to shape individuals to your values by hiring people without a lot of experience in the field and training them up to meet your needs. By enlisting a balanced mix of experienced and inexperienced members, you'll be able to forge an effective team. You are looking for individuals who bring a good mix of skills to the table in fields such as sales, marketing, business development, product development, and product-specific knowledge.

- Look for clues to show that the person you're interviewing for a position truly knows the position. You can figure this out by checking their references, asking scenario-based questions, and by checking their responses to position-specific jargon.

- Look for intelligent people who have a drive for learning and are more interested in success than in making money. While money is a huge motivator for many people, business teams that focuses more on delivering amazing products or services regardless of how much money is at stake will be more successful overall.

- You should also look for somebody who will mesh well with your existing personnel. Even if you come across the most talented prospective employee, a bad attitude or values that are at odds with your company's definition could actually work against your success. Despite the great talent an individual can bring to the table, if the person can't support your basic business premise, your working relationship will be short-lived at best; at worst, it could undermine the foundation of your business.

- Test your candidates before you make a final hiring decision. This can be especially helpful if you are hiring independent contractors. When I was doing freelance work, the majority of my prospective clients asked me to submit a test or a sample of my work before they agreed to hire me. Any sort of test or evaluation will allow you to measure important factors that will influence your business. If a candidate can work under pressure, deliver quality results within a given time frame, and keep promises, at the same time possessing character qualities in line with the key values of your business, you probably have a keeper.

- Don't be afraid to fire somebody if they are not working out. Firing someone may not mean they're a horrible employee. The person could be exceptionally talented, but may just not be the right match for your company. You shouldn't keep somebody on board if he or she isn't helping your company grow.

Be gentle in the way you go about communicating layoffs. If an individual is highly talented, offer to write a letter of recommendation or otherwise provide positive support. In addition to offering valuable assistance, a recommendation letter will reinforce your positive opinion of the employee.

Creating An Advisory Board

An advisory board is a panel made up of several experienced businesspersons who are willing to act as mentors for your startup. They must be completely separate from your organization and will have no shares in your business. Your advisory board exists to provide you with advice, guidance, networking suggestions, and anything else you will need to consider as a first-time entrepreneur. Members of an advisory board often meet with the owners of a business on a quarterly basis, although you can meet as regularly or as infrequently as you need. An advisory board can usually help you gauge the validity of your choices and can serve as a sounding board at times. Advisory boards are not a requirement, but since they can be very helpful, they're highly recommended.

The best kind of advisory board consists of people who have experience in areas of business where you are lacking. For example, if you have no marketing experience, you can benefit immensely by an advisor with a strong background in marketing. As your startup grows, your advisory board can grow and change, as well.

Advisory board members usually serve for a mutually agreed time frame. At the end of that time, you will re-evaluate your needs and choose to re-appoint that member or not. As you bring on board additional employees with the skills of your advisory board members, you may no longer require the services of some of your board members. On the other hand, if you expand your operation to include specific forms of marketing with which none of your team is familiar, you may want to seek out someone with this expertise that you can add to your advisory board.

You'll want to balance the skills and knowledge of your advisory board members with the capabilities of your team to create synergy and lead to success. You should also be on the lookout for advisors who are not afraid to challenge you and who are willing to tell you bluntly the truths they know you don't want to hear. After all, if your board consists of members who are in constant agreement with you, what is the point of having a board?

Qualities To Look For

Like your team members, your board members should be passionate about your business vision and your product. You can identify prospective candidates' passions by paying attention to how interested they appear when you're talking about your business. It's only natural for someone skilled in your industry to have an affinity for what you're intending to accomplish.

It also doesn't hurt if the person is well-known to your industry. Appointing a known expert provides you with the best guidance available and makes your business look great from the outside. There are no rules regarding the size of an advisory board but it generally consists of an odd number of members, most often five to nine in size. The size, however is secondary to the quality of your board members

Focus more on the quality than the quantity of your board. You could have the world's smallest advisory board, but you'll be ahead if it consists of the best possible advisors. Since the process of finding people who are willing to join your advisory board can be tricky, it is best to create a short-list of 10 to 20 candidates. From this list, you will generally have success with about half the number you aim for. Don't be afraid to approach people who may seem impossible to get in touch with; you never know who will be willing to help you!

If you already have a mentor or two who have been giving you casual advice, you may consider asking them to become part of your advisory board. Asking individuals you are already familiar with is easy; you can simply say, "You've already been providing me with great advice; would you like to join my advisory board?" Odds are, the individual will agree.

Approaching individuals you are not already on a comfortable conversational level with may be a bit more difficult. Yet, it can be as easy as offering to buy the prospective candidate a cup of coffee. Use this meeting to get to know each other and to evaluate the person's character and qualifications on an informal level. Later, if you get along well, you can offer your invitation to join the board.

Commitment Level

Remember – being a board member means being able to make a commitment. If you don't hear back from a prospective candidate, it usually indicates that the individual lacks the time to make an additional commitment. If you find a prospective candidate who is able to meet with you on several occasions, you may have discovered someone with the time, and possibly enough interest to be a part of your board.

I recommend you meet with a prospective candidate at least twice before issuing an invitation to join your board. If your potential candidate seems interested, then you can lay out the specifics of what you're looking for, and clearly describe what a commitment to you and your new venture will entail. Listen carefully to any questions and suggestions; remember, you are building a relationship, something that will require some give and take between both of you if you want it to endure.

Once you have successfully developed your advisory board, it is wise to have your lawyer help you draw up a non-disclosure agreement that will adequately protect any confidential information discussed in your meetings.

In terms of compensation, you have several choices. Most advisory board members do not expect any compensation, because they are genuinely interested in helping you succeed. However, you can choose to compensate your board members for their time and resources to express your gratitude for their services or to motivate them to continue and work with you.

Although members of an advisory board do not hold shares in your business as do members of a director's board, you can choose the option of providing your board members with a small percentage of equity. You could also offer to pay for travel costs and/or provide free food at your meetings (I don't know about you, but free food almost always motivates me!).

Chapter 9: Your Customer Service Strategy

As your startup begins to come to life you will likely notice you're still missing a really important piece: **customer service**. As a consumer, you probably already know the value of good customer service. Can you recall a time in your life where you had a bad experience trying to return a product you purchased? Perhaps you found it almost impossible to get hold of a customer service representative, only to receive rude service when you finally reached someone, or unsatisfying results, or even worse – a dead end. Can you also recall a time you've been blown away by incredible customer service that extended above and beyond your expectations, even your desires?

Customer service is vitally important because it helps to shape the perception of your brand. It can also supply important feedback and spark ideas that will make your product and your operations even more attractive to customers. If you want your startup to grow into an established company, a customer service strategy is something you don't want to miss.

One mistake startup businesses often make is to delay thinking about the customer service experience until a customer actually needs service. No, the customer service experience begins as soon as your customer comes into contact with you, whether online or in person. For brick and mortar shops, the experience would begin as soon as a customer opens the door and encounters the atmosphere within, followed (we hope, instantaneously) by a friendly greeting. With an online business, a personalized greeting is a positive example of customer service.

You want to give your customers a great first impression. Then, you want to follow through with an excellent product and ongoing attention for its use and care. Waiting for a problem to arise before you show a customer you care, will probably result in losing that customer.

Personalize Your Interactions

Customers enjoy attention directed toward them, personally. It's easy for people to tell when you're dishing out a generic response. Of course, it's good to know what to say when a customer comes to you with a specific problem, but you want to tailor your response to the specific customer. Call your customers by their first names when you can and get to know as much as about them as possible so you can speak to their unique circumstances.

Take advantage of the many existing customer service tools available on your website or social media pages. One of the basic levels of customer service is the well-known Frequently Asked Questions (FAQ) page. This page responds to some of the most common customer service questions you will encounter. A FAQ page that addresses these most common issues can spare your customers excessive wait time for a response by providing easy solutions. As part of your website content, you can even post directional or informative articles, video guides, or anything else that can help your customers and attract traffic to your site through search engine optimization. If you have product or service descriptions on your website, see to it that each description is explained fully and clearly, leaving no unanswered questions.

You should put together your customer service strategy before you launch your business. As soon as customers run into snags, they'll come to you, expecting to have a solution waiting for them.

When I was a young adult, I spent some time working at a fast food restaurant. One night, a customer called to notify me that we had forgotten to put his French fries in his bag, and he had driven off without them. The next thing he asked me was, "So what can you do about this?" I was still slightly inexperienced in providing excellent customer service, so I choked on this question and eventually stammered out, "Well, I could take your name down and next time you come I could give you a refund or you can get a free fry." The customer responded with, "How about giving me a refund in addition to a free fry?" I agreed and only wished I had thought of that in the first place, instead of needing the customer to lead me to the solution.

This is a good example of what happens when a customer puts you on the spot with a problem. When you don't have a solution already thought out, it can make your business look weak and unprepared. However, when you *do* have a solution waiting, it will leave a much better impression.

Building A Great Customer Service Team

- Prepare your customer service team to face irate customers; give them the tools they need to defuse a customer's anger. The last thing you need is a team member who mirrors the angry customer. Customer service is not always pleasant and easy; it requires tons of patience, along with a willingness to identify with the customer and address even unspoken underlying needs.

- Customer service team members will need to demonstrate great communication skills. They should be able to fully and clearly explain things to customers to avoid any miscommunication or to give out the wrong idea. They should be able to demonstrate active listening skills versus just hearing. Your team members should be well-versed in your business. After all, if your customer service team doesn't know what they are talking about, how can they help convert an angry customer into a satisfied one?

- Your most valuable customer service skill is the ability to develop rapport with others. When an angry customer is able to connect, on a personal level, with a team member, then you will be able to turn around a bad situation; the customer may well leave with a new level of appreciation for your business.

- Great customer service consistently replaces negative statements with positive terms. If a product isn't available, don't just say "Sorry, it's not available." Instead, shape your response in the form of a <u>positive statement</u> such as, "That product will be available within two weeks." In addition to giving customers hope that their desires will indeed be satisfied, you are reframing their reality in a positive light. It's good psychology as well as quality customer service.

- Give your customers real answers. Avoid responses that don't really tell your customer anything. Offer them the most complete information possible that doesn't leave them with unanswered questions.

Customer service is a two-way street. When your customers approach you they feel a lot better when you welcome them in. In turn, you will want to also move willingly toward your customers. Don't leave them hanging in the dark, all alone; let them know they have an ally in you.

People like to know what's going on. If you're opening a second location for your business, it is best to announce it to your audience. A simple announcement on your website or social media page can go a long way toward alleviating any anxiety caused by changes in the way you operate. At the same time, you're strengthening the image of your company as a successful firm. After all, you've gotta be doing well if you can open up a new location!

Customers who live near your new location will get a real boost; it means a lot that you care enough to bring your products closer to *them*! Make the most of this opportunity to build on that added confidence in your brand; add new customers with neighborhood-targeted marketing and extend a special invitation to existing customers to make themselves at home in the new space.

If you're coming out with something new, let your customers in on it and get them excited. Don't wait for the product or service to become available for purchase; you can build enthusiasm even before the launch with well-placed teasers, blog posts, and news releases. Have fun with it. Hold contests to help pick a name, give away advance samples, and encourage customer feedback.

As soon as the new product is launched, encourage your customers to help you spread the word by uploading selfies with the new product on social media. Stirring up customer engagement is key to developing a strong sense of customer service. Customers bond with the product to the point of claiming ownership of it.

Customer engagement also reaches your customers on a most basic level. One of our deepest needs is to be heard. When you interact with customers on a personal level, they feel like they're truly being heard, and this strengthens their ties to you, your business, and your products.

Important Customer Service Tips

- Many consumers value human interaction, especially in a world where many businesses rely on automated customer service methods. Have you ever tried getting hold of a company only to find yourself frustrated after pushing buttons that lead to dead ends or even worse, the dreaded voice-activated answering machine, where you can say "yes" a hundred times only to hear a monotone voice reply, "I'm sorry, I didn't understand that."

  Since most businesses let computers handle customer service, you can stand out by providing it the "old fashioned way." Have a real person answer the phone for a change. While you may struggle to find a way to add in another salary to your budget, it can be very worthwhile to offer live support.

  Of course, it is still important to integrate advanced technology into your customer service strategy. Many companies encourage their customers to provide feedback. However, many customers look for another human to help them through their troubles.

It is important to respond to your customers when they offer feedback. There is nothing more frustrating than attempting to contact a company only to get no reply in return. A non-response communicates that you don't care. If a customer gives you a compliment, a simple "Thanks for your feedback, (insert name here)" can work wonders!

- Offer your customer multiple ways to get in touch with you. Some people prefer talking to a live person on the phone while others prefer writing an email or visiting in person. Some will only contact you via social media. Do everything you can to make it easy for customers to access your contact information. There's nothing worse than being unable to find a phone number within a couple clicks.

- Train all employees who have the slightest chance of interacting with a customer in the acceptable way to respond to customer complaints. Tell them explicitly how you want them to respond to each anticipated problem. Then give them a plan to follow for *unanticipated* problems! Don't wait until a problem arises and then start scrambling for a response.

  View this as just another step toward being prepared. You want your customers to be able to easily reach a customer service specialist who exudes calm confidence in tackling the problem, whatever it is. Ideally, your customer service specialists will be able to spot potential problems and work out practical preventative solutions well before they can become problems in reality. This is <u>the best kind of problem to have</u>.

- Train yourself and your staff to never become defensive toward a customer who expresses a problem or recounts or a bad experience, even if their story seems fanciful and farfetched. I can't tell you how many times I've read reviews for a business that note the business owner attacked anyone who described a problem or a bad experience. Defensiveness is unprofessional and will not encourage others do business with you.

I can recall an example of this from my personal experience working in retail. One day, an elderly man brought in a package of lightbulbs to return them. The problem was, we had never sold that brand, ever. I tried to explain this to the customer and even suggesting he might have purchased them in the store next door, but he was adamant, insisting they had come from *my* store.

I didn't know what to do, especially since our computers couldn't even read the barcode on the package. I ended up calling my district manager who instructed me to give the man a refund, even though it wasn't our product. That was a wise response. The district manager chose to act in a way that would give the customer a positive experience, enabling him to walk out of our store satisfied and much more likely to rely on us again than if we had rejected his claim outright.

- Look for ways to respond to customer service inquiries as quickly as possible, without sacrificing quality. We live in a fast-paced world where the people tend to have little patience – even less patience when they are feeling frustrated – so the faster you can help them resolve their issues, the better impression you leave them with.

- Your customer service strategy can even generate money for you. For example, if your average response time is 48 hours for all customer enquiries you can instead use that time to offer the customer an upsell. Of course, you shouldn't exchange a faster response time by itself for money, but you could include it as a part of a package deal.

Some companies offer advanced memberships or packages that provide bigger and better services and options to customers who are willing to pay a little more for the added value. You can also guarantee a faster response time to these customers as part of the package deal.

- When interacting with a customer, always use it as an opportunity to show your appreciation for the customer's business. Sometimes a simple "thank you" can go a long way!

- Don't wait for your customers to come to you. Take them by surprise and come to them! If your customer base is small enough to do this, pick up the phone and call the customer directly. Ask how he is doing, wish her a happy birthday, call to say "happy holidays," or anything that has nothing to do with buying from you.

  This works with employees as well. When I worked as a manager in retail, I constantly felt like I only called my employees to ask them to come in on their days off. Before long I felt like a really annoying boss who only contacted people when I wanted something. So I began an experiment. I would call employees just to wish them a great day, a positive morning, or encourage them to enjoy their day off. The results were great! My employees were absolutely floored to know I cared.

  One morning, I called an employee to tell her I hoped she would have a great morning and that I'd see her at one p.m. When she came in later that day, I asked what she thought of my phone call. She told me that when she saw my name on her phone, she thought I was going to ask her to come in early but she was shocked to find out that I wasn't; it really made her day.

  Although this experiment is unrelated to buying and selling, you can still see how important it is to remember that your customers – and your employees – are human. If you only contact them when you're trying to make a buck, they will notice it and feel like you're trying to use them for your own gain. I'm sure that's not what you intend.

- Treat your employees well and their pleasure will flow through them to your customers. Unhappy employees are less likely to put their best effort into their work. On the other hand, employees who are happy and feel a connection to their employer and loyalty to your brand are more likely to pass that positive energy on to customers.

Make customer service an important part of your work culture and company mission statement. The earlier you start placing a strong emphasis on promoting customer – and employee – satisfaction, the sooner you will begin to see great results.

Chapter 10: Common Legal Issues For Startups

You're almost there! However, before you launch your startup you should educate yourself on the legalities of doing business. There are many external legal factors to consider, things like filing for business insurance and paying taxes. There are also many internal legal factors you definitely don't want to skip, because they'll avoid problems for you down the road.

When it comes to hiring lawyers and accountants, never sacrifice quality for quantity! Don't settle for the services of somebody who may be cheaper but has less experience in your type of business. You want to hire someone who truly knows business law, tax law, and all the rules and regulations of the business world. You will rely on your lawyer and accountant to spot potential trouble and help you head them off before they become expensive and dangerous. In the next few pages, you will learn some of the basic, yet important, legal issues involved in launching a startup.

Internal Legalities

Contracts – Although they may seem unnecessary, legal experts highly recommend you establish a written contract between yourself and anybody you do business with. This is basic preventative maintenance. When you have the terms down in black and white, nobody can claim they deserve a bigger percentage of profits or they have all the time in the world to produce what you need. Even a simple handwritten contractual agreement will avoid any sticky "he said/she said" conversations down the road.

A contract between co-founders is needed to establish clear ownership rights and to clearly divide up the responsibilities of the venture. It will include information on salaries, liability, and who gets what percentage of sales or shares. You will identify each founder and describe his or her function within the business. This can prevent arguments over internal responsibilities, as well as declaring clear lines of liability, just in case there is trouble.

You will also need signed contracts for all work you hire with an independent contractor. This type of contract will define payment rates and clearly define the work to be performed. If necessary, it will include a statement of nondisclosure, so you can protect proprietary aspects of your business.

You can even make a contract of sorts between yourself and your customers. A car dealer may require a contract entitling the customer to free maintenance up to a hundred thousand miles, also stating that the dealer is not liable for car damage if the customer fails to keep up with regular maintenance.

Contracts can be as long and involved as necessary, but they must be clear and easy to understand by all parties. For basic issues, you can find contract templates on the internet. Once you have retained an attorney, your lawyer can assist you in the creation of all the basic contract templates you will need. Your attorney will see to it that all bases are covered between you and whatever party you're dealing with.

Non-Disclosure Agreements – Non-disclosure agreements, or NDAs, are common in business today. An NDA is a contract that prevents a person with access to your confidential business information from sharing it with anyone else, on pain of legal consequences. This is most commonly used with vendors, but you may also require your employees to sign an NDA as part of the onboarding process.

Company Bylaws – Your company bylaws are an informal set of rules used to govern the members within an organization. They act as an "employee handbook" for members of upper management. You can utilize bylaws to set the standards for appointing board members, making changes to the budget, or anything related to the internal workings of the organization.

While there are no laws requiring you to create company bylaws, it's definitely not something you should skip.

Employee Files

When you hire employees to work on payroll there are a couple important legal steps you must take to comply with federal and state law. When hiring a new employee, you must provide them with important tax documents to complete, such as a W-4 (the standard tax withholding form) and an I-9 form (identity verification). If the employee is not an independent contractor, he or she should also receive and sign an "at-will" document, which enables either party to terminate employment at any time for any reason.

You may need to collect and store an employee's personal information for benefit eligibility. You should also have your employees read and sign off on an employee handbook, which outlines the terms and policies of employment and serves as a contract.

For your part, you will see to it that your hiring practices are non-discriminatory, per the Equal Opportunity Act. If you plan on offering stock to employees, you should also have your lawyer help you provide your employees with the important information on purchasing stock shares, as well as other documentation required by law.

External Legalities

Stock Security – According to federal and state law, all corporations, LLCs, and limited partnerships must follow specific disclosure laws when selling stock to any third-party interests. If you do not follow this law, your business can be hit with severe fines, and you will have to purchase back all the stocks you sold. Your lawyer can help you navigate these legalities.

Taxation – Taxation is an essential area of business law. You definitely don't want to mess this up. How many times have you read an article in your local newspaper about a business owner in trouble for tax evasion or tax fraud? When you don't take your business taxes seriously, it can lead to serious repercussions. Fortunately, your accountant will be there to give you the necessary advice on the taxes you are liable for and can set up a schedule to ensure that you are setting aside the appropriate funds to cover your financial obligations.

As we discussed earlier in this book, the business structure you adopt has unique rules regarding how your business is taxed. Depending on your type of business and the state out of which you operate, you may be required to pay sales tax, estimated quarterly tax, and any number of miscellaneous local taxes. Again, your accountant is the best person to help you navigate these requirements. Your accountant will also be able to help you when it comes to stock sales and their taxation.

Digital World Legalities – When your business is active online, there are some more laws that you must abide by to ensure that you are protected in the digital world. When it comes to digital legalities, the greatest concern is your terms of use and the privacy policy on your website. Go to your favorite company's website right now and I guarantee you will see a link that directs you to their terms of agreement and their privacy policy.

Most states require you to include these two things on your website by law. A **terms of agreement** page is basically a contract between the business and the user or customer that limits liability to the business. A typical **terms of service** statement includes information on intellectual property, dispute resolutions, and any necessary disclaimers. It sometimes will also include return policy information.

The purpose of a **privacy policy** is to disclose what you do with users' information. A typical privacy policy discloses how and what kind of user information your site collects, whether that information will be shared or sold, how your information may be integrated with a separate website (i.e. YouTube or Pinterest), how your cookies interact with the site, and how the business protects the information collected by the site. If applicable, the site may also contain a policy for underage users. Since each business is different, there are no universal terms of agreement or privacy policy to simply copy and paste into your website. Your lawyer will be able to help you draft the statements that are best suited to your needs.

Insurance – Insuring your business is just about as important as insuring your home, car, life, or anything else of great value. Business insurance is expensive, but it can also be expensive if you do *not* protect your assets. The main consequence of not purchasing adequate business insurance is that your business will use its profits to cover any damages, physical or legal. If your profits are not sufficient to cover the damages, you may end up dipping into your personal savings.

Depending on the type of business you operate, your state or local jurisdiction may even require you to purchase insurance before you can open your doors to customers. While some business structures already come with limited liability provisions, this generally doesn't cover catastrophic events or insurance for internal operations.

Types Of Business Insurance

Liability insurance, is your basic, most essential form of business insurance. This is all the more important if your place of business and whatever you are selling poses a potential physical risk to your customers. General liability insurance can help you cover most, if not all, of the damages in the event that your business or product injured a customer or damaged their personal possessions. Professional liability service protects you from errors and accidents that may occur, including accusations of malpractice.

Even if you require your customers to sign a liability waiver, you will still need some liability insurance, just to handle unanticipated events. For example, if somebody trips on the sidewalk outside of your office and is injured, the injured party could sue your business for physical damages. What if one of your products is faulty and explodes, injuring a customer or damaging property? You could be held responsible for the damage. Although you will never purposefully hurt anyone or damage their possessions, the reality is that accidents happen. Liability insurance is there to protect you from this sort of damage.

You will also require liability insurance to deal with the few individuals out there who are eager to sue your business on the basis of trumped-up or imagined wrongs. If you keep up with the news, you've probably seen plenty of examples. A few years ago, a man sued a sub shop for false advertising when he bought an advertised 12-inch sub that turned out to measure a couple inches too short. I remember thinking it would have never crossed my mind to measure the actual sandwich, but someone out there certainly did, and chose to hold it against a company.

Theft or **commercial property insurance** protects the physical aspects of your business. In the event that the physical location of your business is burglarized or held up, theft insurance can help cover the costs of replacing whatever was broken or stolen. Startups with a brand new location are at the highest risk of experiencing a burglary or break-in. A new site is highly attractive because the location will be filled with brand new equipment, offering a high resale value.

Commercial property insurance can protect your business in the event of an accident or an event that is out of anyone's control. In the event of a fire, a tornado or other freak accident that destroys your location and resources, property insurance can help cover the replacement of your property without jeopardizing your business. You can also purchase <u>business interruption insurance</u> to replace lost sales during any time you are unable to do business due to losing access to your physical location.

If your business employs others, you will need to purchase **Workman's Compensation insurance**. Workman's comp is a type of insurance required by law. It will protect your business in the event that one of your employees is injured on the job.

Employees who are injured and can't work as a result, are able to receive a percentage of their normal salary during the time they are out of work. Workman's compensation insurance will enable the employee to receive medical and rehabilitative treatment fully covered by the business.

If you run your startup out of your home and an accident occurs, your normal home insurance policy may not cover the damages. For example, if you're running a technology startup out of your garage and one of the computers you use for business purposes sparks and sets fire to your garage, the damages to your personal property may not be covered, unless you have purchased home-based business insurance.

If the nature of your startup includes driving a vehicle, it is important to look into purchasing **commercial car insurance**. Commercial car insurance is just like regular car insurance, but it generally will protect any products or equipment you're carrying inside the vehicle.

Don't worry; you won't need to purchase every type of insurance we've talked about in the first days of your business. Depending on the kind of business you own, you can choose the insurance that will best protect you. While you will probably require liability insurance, you may not need home-based insurance. Many insurance companies offer a business owner's package that includes multiple types of protection. It is generally much cheaper to bundle your insurance policies with a single insurance company than to buy individual policies piecemeal from multiple sources.

Intellectual Property

Intellectual property is the creative work associated with your business. It includes your name, logo, and proprietary aspects of your business process. It also protects things like an author's writing, to which the original creator holds the rights. It is important to ensure the protection of your intellectual property because, not only is it a valuable result of your creativity, it may also become increasingly valuable as your company grows. Potential investors will view this protection as an indication that you take your business seriously; they will view it as a form of leverage on the competition.

One of the most serious mistakes a startup entrepreneur can make when it comes to intellectual property is to underplay its importance. Since proper protection of your intellectual property can take some time to establish, you'll want to act as soon as you have developed something you know you will use. As with other legal issues, it is best to engage a lawyer skilled in intellectual property rights to walk you through this process.

The three main types of intellectual property are patents, trademarks, and copyrights.

Patents

A patent protects you from other people manufacturing, using, or selling your invention. For a specified amount of time it gives you the sole rights to the use of your unique product. This gives you a competitive edge within your market, so make the best use of patent protection while you have this unique advantage over the competition.

You can use a patent to protect a physical invention, a product or service feature, a product design, or even a unique approach to a process or procedure. The best practice is to file for any necessary patents well before you publically release your product or service; otherwise it will be at risk for theft. The patent process is pretty complex, so it's important to leave yourself enough time to patent items before their launch.

The good news about patents in the United States is that you can often use a fast-track option to speed up the patent approval process, in exchange – of course – for a fee. The benefit of utilizing this program is that you will wait significantly less time for your patent to be approved, making it easier to use your new product and to register a patent overseas.

Trademarks

A trademark is a logo, design, or identity – such as a brand – that causes your product or service to stand out from its generic version. As long as the trademark you want to use isn't in active use by anyone else (which you can find out by doing a trademark search), you can register and use any trademark you want for your business. Registering your trademark prevents others from copying – and benefitting from – your brand.

Copyrights

A copyright prevents third parties from reproducing an original article, book, song, or movie. Others are not allowed to use an item you've created in any form of expression without your explicit permission. To this end, you'll want to keep a record of your creation dates. This will become all-important if anyone else claims to have created something before you have published it. Luckily, most creative works are developed on a computer; your computer file, showing its date of creation, will usually suffice to prove prior ownership.

At the same time, you will want to ensure you are not violating any copyright laws in the process of conducting your own business. The most common example is the use of a photograph taken by someone else, without obtaining permission from the source. Before you use any type of intellectual property that does not originate with your company, you – or your lawyer – should perform a clearance search to prove that the rights to it are available.

Patents, trademarks, and copyrights you register in the United States are only valid in the United States. If you outsource work from another country, it is a good idea to establish contracts to further protect your ideas or inventions internationally.

Intellectual Property Strategy

You'll want to work with your team to create an intellectual property strategy. It can be costly and a waste of time to protect everything. Don't patent your intellectual property too soon. This will reduce the amount of time you have unfettered rights to your product.

Give your team six months to a year to figure out what products, services, or ideas will put your startup in the best position. Then move to protect those specific items.

The best way to begin developing an intellectual property strategy is to create a list of all the ideas and tangibles that qualify as intellectual property. Working from that list, you can then determine which items will call for a patent, a trademark, or a copyright, as opposed to items you can protect through contracts, confidentiality agreements, encryption, or other methods that are less complex.

Chapter 11: Funding Your Venture

Before you can bring your startup to life, odds are you will need some type of funding or financial assistance to help you get started. The good news is that there are several methods of funding available for startup entrepreneurs. Each type of funding comes with unique benefits as well as specific potential drawbacks, so you'll be wise to weigh their advantages and disadvantages before you commit to a specific form of funding.

Loans And Credit Lines

The first business funding option comes through a bank loan or a line of business credit. The benefit of turning to a bank loan or line of credit is that when you receive the funding, you have the freedom to spend it however you wish (on business expenses, of course). With a bank loan or line of credit, you are not required to share any ownership of your startup with the bank. Bank loans tend to have low interest rates and you'll find that your credit limits will tend to be high.

The main drawback to this form of funding is that banks tend to hesitate to approve these options for new businesses or individuals who lack a past positive business history. Of course, this type of funding isn't impossible to obtain. It helps to have a solid business plan you can present to your bank officer. Funding through a bank will also require considerable paperwork and a will include a long application process. Many first-time entrepreneurs find it all overwhelming, so be prepared to exercise considerable patience throughout the process.

Investors

Another common method of funding is through investors. This would include close friends or family members who are willing to put money into your startup.

You can also seek out third-party investors. The main sources of third-party investment are venture capitalists and angel investors.

Venture capitalists are an ideal source of funding for startup entrepreneurs. These individuals are willing to invest their money into startups, regardless the owner's experience level. Venture capitalists rely on the hope that your startup will be wildly successful and they will receive a significant return on their dollar.

You can often find venture capitalists through professional associations, networking, or via a simple Internet search. Before you decide to settle down with a venture capitalist, it is always best to do your homework. Check out the individual's track record and ask to see references from other successful ventures they have backed in the past. Many venture capitalists are professional investors, but it can never hurt to do your research.

Angel investors are like venture capitalists in the sense that they provide financial support to a new business. The difference is, angel investors contribute funds in exchange for a piece of ownership, such as a free t-shirt with your logo, a free copy of your book, or another valued product related to your business. Family and close friends often fall into the category of angel investors.

Crowdfunding

Crowdfunding is a relatively new form of funding that has helped numerous businesses get off the ground. It consists of presenting your idea to potential customers via an online platform that allows anyone who supports the idea to donate money toward the startup until it reaches its funding goal.

A startup can incentivize donations by promising the donor a small reward in exchange for the money contributed. Better and more elaborate rewards tend to come with higher donations. Crowdfunding is a highly competitive method of funding; it can be very hit-or-miss, but it's a great way to test out a product's potential in specific markets.

Most crowdfunding websites enable their users to integrate marketing methods as part of the crowdfunding effort, making it easy to connect to other social media platforms. You'll want to carefully plan out a marketing strategy that will help you stand out from everybody else.

Some businesses have seen much success in crowdfunding. The popular party game "Cards Against Humanity" began as a Kickstarter campaign, where it was originally offered as a free download. Based on the success of the Kickstarter campaign, it became a physical game with actual cards.

Bootstrapping

Bootstrapping is a term that describes an entrepreneur who launches a business with personal funds or from the initial profits of pre-orders. The main benefit of bootstrapping is that the business owner can operate a business without any input from – or meddling by – outside investors.

The main drawback of bootstrapping is that it can be a risky personal investment. If an entrepreneur spends an entire life savings on the business and it fails, all of that money is gone. Additionally, the success of your business may be limited to the amount of money you can personally invest.

If your startup is structured as a partnership, you and your partner can each invest some personal savings into the business. However, the main risks associated with such an arrangement include possible disagreements over how the business is run and what to do if one partner wants to withdraw from the venture. If you combine a partnership with bootstrapping, it is important to draw up clear contracts that lay out terms that both you and your partners agree upon.

Grant Funding

Government grants are another option for funding that you may find useful. There are many grants available from the government. Government agencies will give out grants in hopes that your business will help to stimulate the economy. The major drawback of these grants is that it can take a long time for them to be processed and actually appear in your hands. The benefit, however, is that it won't cost a thing beyond the time and effort necessary to complete the application.

Grants are also offered by private foundations for various reasons. If you are a military veteran or a woman you may find targeted grants that will help you get started in business. Each grant will have its own focus or purpose. It may take a little research, but you may well find one that applies perfectly to your situation.

A small business office may be able to help you find local foundations to apply for. Your library may also have a section devoted to small businesses that will include information on applying for grants; just ask a librarian for assistance. You can also search for applicable grants at www.grants.gov.

Other Resources

You can always enter a ***contest*** to help fund your venture, if you can find one that is relevant and applies to you. Large, well-established companies often offer contests where you can win money to use toward funding a business in exchange for writing an essay or proving that your business idea is really awesome and helpful.

The good news for startups is that there are many resources available to help you get started. The key is finding local resources that are appropriate to address your needs.

Local Organizations

Check around with your local educational institutions and community development groups and associations. Many community colleges offer assistance to small businesses. Some towns offer financial incentives to businesses that want to operate in their communities, so it's also best to check in with your local government and the Chamber of Commerce to see what resources are available to you.

Many communities have local SCORE chapters. SCORE is an organization where retired or well-seasoned business leaders volunteer their time to mentor and provide free guidance to new entrepreneurs. I utilized their services myself as a new business owner and was highly satisfied with the help I received.

Space Sharing

Many larger cities offer co-working space. These are essentially short-term office space you rent and share with other entrepreneurs. Co-working fosters networking and can help you get your startup going, especially in the early days before you are able to procure your own office or meeting space. In addition to providing working space and interaction with other professionals, it serves as a physical location where you can host clients and meet with potential investors. Your presence in a physical space lends credibility to the reality of your business and can become a strong selling point with potential investors.

Bartering

One creative way to get help with the funding of your startup is to barter. The bartering of services can often protect your budget while allowing you to obtain some of the services you need. For example, a freelance writer could provide article-writing services to an accountant in exchange for financial reporting services. Although bartering is not widely used for startup funding, it can definitely be an appealing area to explore. If you're going to barter services, I recommend that you also read up on what it entails when you file your business taxes. You may be required to treat the services exchanged as income; your accountant can give you the details.

Self-Funding

Other, less-than-optimal funding strategies include borrowing money from your 401k or cashing out your life insurance policy. Because these options can wield major negative consequences on your life, they may not be worth the considerable risk they entail. If your business does not succeed, you will have no way to recover those funds; they will be lost forever.

Chapter 12: Financial Planning

Obtaining funding is only the beginning of your financial responsibility. Financial planning is the process of ensuring that you are putting the money allocated for your startup to the most efficient use, once you have enough money to actually launch. When you know how your well your money is working for you, it enables you to make better decisions for your startup.

One of the top reasons many startups fail within their first year is due to financial issues. It is usually difficult for startups to financially plan their first year because they have no historical data to use to help them gauge their success.

The Start Of A Budget

When it comes to financial planning, the first thing you should do is create an overall budget for your startup. A few chapters ago, we discussed how to create a marketing budget. The process of creating an overall budget is similar. It will include every cost that concerns your startup.

Tracking Your Costs

The first step in creating a budget is to know how much money you have to work with. For example, if you took out a bank loan of $100,000 to put toward one year of building your startup, that will be your starting amount.

Next, you should open up a blank document and create two sections: **fixed costs** and **variable costs**. Fixed costs are expenses that are likely to remain the same over a long period of time, such as facility rental. Variable costs are expenses that are more likely to fluctuate from month to month, such as electricity or the cost of a material you will use to build your product.

List the most obvious expenses you'll incur over a one-year period. Allow yourself enough padding so that none of your expenses will push you over your starting amount. For example, if your starting amount is $100,000 and your expenses come out to $150,000, you will need find a way either to cut back on your spending or to increase your starting amount. You can check around with suppliers for less costly materials or find a way to generate the extra funding.

Expense Categories

While the expenses of each individual business will differ, there are many common expenses that most startups will likely incur. These include:

- Marketing costs (market research, product development, marketing methods, etc.).

- Borrowing (loans, credits, etc.).

- Initial inventory.

- Technology.

- Decorating, interior or exterior design.

- Business software.

- Furniture.

- Digital design (logo, website, etc.).

- Equipment.

- Internet service.

- Employee wages.

- Registering trademarks/patents/copyrights.

- Money for your cash registers, if applicable.

- Insurance.

- Quarterly estimated tax. When you're in business for yourself, there is no government withholding, so you must be responsible for paying your own portion of taxes to the government.

- Rent and utilities.

- Permits.

- Phone lines.

- Professional services, including retaining an attorney and an accountant.

- Business cards.

- Office and cleaning supplies.

- Website fees.

It is also always a great idea to budget for unforeseen expenses that may crop up. In the business world, you never know what kind of expenses you will incur, so a little padding is in order. You should also understand the difference between an **expense** and an **asset**. Expenses are things that are used up and have no residual value. An asset is something you purchase for your business and, even if it depreciates in value over time, it will retain some value. The two are treated very differently at tax time. Your accountant will be able to guide you when it comes to reporting your expenses and assets appropriately.

Sales Forecasting

The next step of financial planning is to predict the numbers that pertain to your first few years of sales. While you cannot magically predict what your sales, customer counts, or other sales-related numbers will be, there is usually enough public material available to help you create a sales **forecast.** A forecast is a prediction of how much money your startup expects to make, how many products you will sell, and how many customers you will acquire within a certain timeframe. Many startups create a three-year forecast to get started. After that time, you will have actual data to draw upon; then your forecasting will become much more accurate and trustworthy.

The best way to create a sales forecast is to start by looking at businesses in your industry that are comparable to your own. If you have worked in this industry before, you likely have a general idea of what to expect. Similarly, you could find a mentor who has owned a similar business and ask that person to help you create a forecast.

Your accountant can be a great source of information, as well. Accountants generally have multiple clients and their experience in your industry can make them accurate judges of your potential profits and expenses.

After your first year in operation, you can review your numbers to see how well your startup has performed, compared to your estimations. If your performance numbers are lower than what you were aiming for, you will need to make cost cutbacks while you adjust your forecast going forward. At the same time, you'll want to review your business to find ways to boost those numbers in the future. If your numbers show that you achieved results beyond what you were aiming for, you can adjust your forecasts upward and possibly begin to think about expansion options.

Startup Costs

Thinking in terms of the costs of your startup, you should always try to remain realistic. A new startup will be much smaller, financially, compared to an established company. While it is important to envision the size and scope of your startup in the future, it is important to remember that you have a limited amount of money to invest in your startup. While you may envision having 10 offices throughout the country one day, you'll probably need only one office to begin with. If your funds are truly tight, you will have to accept that your first office might even be located in your basement.

When you first start out, you probably won't need hundreds of printed promotional items, fancy company uniforms, or anything that does not directly relate to the operational portion of your startup. If you find yourself becoming too detailed in your expectations, I recommend making a list of everything you want for your business. Then, separate out the items that are essential to your present operations and set aside everything else for future consideration.

Now that you have pared down your list to everything that is essential, you'll need to budget for these items. You will be able to include those nonessential items in the future, after your startup is consistently profitable, with enough surplus funds to support them.

Other essentials you will need – both to assess the current state of your business and to make financial projections – are the income statement, the balance sheet, and the cash flow statement.

Income Statement

An income statement is a report that reflects your profits and losses by showing how much money you gained through sales and the amount of money you lost through expenses and other means. Most companies publish an income statement once per quarter so they have a general idea of how their money worked for them during that period. As a new startup, you'll want to produce one each month. An income statement should show your total expenses, subtracted from your total operating revenue, which gives you your gross profit.

Once you have your gross profit, you should add up your overhead for the quarter and subtract it from your gross profits to get your operating income. Subtract from your operating income any other expenses you may have incurred; this will give your net profit, or your free and clear profit. You can choose to pour this profit back into your business, or you can spend it otherwise.

Balance Sheet

A balance sheet shows how your liabilities and your stakeholder equities balance out your assets. The purpose of this document is to show where any borrowed money is going. Your assets should equal the sum total of your liabilities and equities. Your assets will include anything physical, such as money and inventory. Some examples of liabilities are rent payments and sales taxes. The simplest way to create a balance sheet is to divide a document in half and list a breakdown of your assets on one side with a total at the bottom and a breakdown of your liabilities and equities on the other side with its total at the bottom. The two numbers at the bottom of the statement should match.

Cash Flow Report

A cash flow sheet is a statement that shows how much cash flows through your business within a certain timeframe. A cash flow sheet should include the cash associated with business operations, investments, and finances. The purpose of a cash flow sheet is to show the total amount of cash coming from these three areas of your business. Startups will forecast the first three months of their cash flow. At the end of the first month of operations, you will create your first cash flow sheet and be able to compare it to your projections for accuracy. You can adjust your future projections as necessary, and then see how well you measure up in the months that follow.

With the help of these three documents, along with an idea of your expenses and a sales forecast that extends out to at least three years, you should be able to successfully plan for your startup costs until you have actual sales and expense data to make forecasting more accurate.

Chapter 13: Preparing to Launch

Once you have covered everything you've discovered in the past few chapters of this book, you're almost ready to launch your startup! I know from experience how exciting it can be to launch a business or release a new book. The most important thing I have learned is that excitement often leads to haste and haste can cause you to overlook important details. That said, I have compiled a checklist you can use to make sure you've covered all the necessary ground before you officially launch your new business.

Pre-Launch Checklist

- Have you invested time into researching your industry to know if there is a strong demand for your products or services? Is your business idea feasible?

- Have you researched and selected an accountant, lawyer, banker, and other important allies?

- Have you thoroughly researched and selected your legal structure?

- Is your business plan completed?

- Have you settled on a name, made sure it is available for use, and purchased an appropriate domain name?

- Have you identified your target audience, created an ideal customer profile, and begun developing your brand and marketing strategy?

- Have you chosen an appropriate business location and does it fit into your budget?

- Have you obtained the right amount of funding?

- Have you identified, planned, and filled all necessary positions on your team? Have you hired the necessary amount of employees?

- Have you developed your customer service strategy, keeping in mind that your customers' experience begins the moment they connect with your business?

- Have you taken steps to protect your intellectual property? Are all contracts written out and signed?

- Have you researched and prepared a three-year sales forecast along with an expense list, income statement, cash flow sheet, and balance sheet?

The Press Release

Assuming that you've got all the bases covered, you're now ready to launch your business! But how do you go about letting the world know you're open for business? Your best bet is going to be through a **press release**. A press release is a one page, well-written statement given to journalists and other news outlets to inform them of a newsworthy story, in this case, your official launch.

When you write a press release, it must be in associated press (AP) format, which is the standard form most news outlets follow. The first couple of lines will tell the reader who you are as a business. It will give your launch date, and will describe why this is important for the world to know. You should include a brief description of your products or services as well as a quote from the founders or business owners.

You will close the statement with an explanation of where your startup stands in relation to its industry and by sketching a brief description of the founders. When you initially introduce a person in your press release, you will include both the first and last name as well as the company title. Thereafter, you can generally refer to an individual by first or last name alone.

You should include a company representative's name and contact information at the end, so that journalists will know who to approach for follow-up information.

Other conventions used in press releases include:

- When describing numbers in text, spell out the words for numbers one to nine and, use numeral notation for over anything from 10 and above.

- Use a single space after each period or other ending punctuation.

- Omit the Oxford comma; this is the final comma before the "and" that ends a list of items.

Publishing Your Press Release

Once you have written your press release (or have hired an experienced press release writer to craft it for you), you can start sending email pitches to news outlets in hopes that they will publish your announcement. You'll want to send out your pitch to as many places as possible. You can also market your launch as an exclusive story to gain the attention of more established news outlets that may want to publish before others. You can also utilize the paid and free press release services available online to boost your chances of exposure.

Once any type of news outlet publishes your story you will have several advantages. The first is that the press release is likely to be published online and, with the right keywords, can serve as a means of attracting customers through search engine optimization. The second advantage is that the online story will have a link you can publish yourself on your company social media pages to gain additional traffic.

The third advantage is that anyone following your company on social media can share the link, further broadening your exposure. Finally, once you have had your first experience with a press release, any future press releases will more easily gain an audience. Keep a press release in mind whenever something huge or new happens within your business; make the most of any business expansion, technological breakthrough, or professional award, maximizing each opportunity to get your name and brand before the public.

Email Announcements

If you have built an email list prior to launching, you can also send out email announcements to your followers announcing that you are ready for business. The most popular and successful way to build an email list is by including an opt-in form on your company website. People hesitate to give out their email address these days, so many businesses will offer them something in exchange for the information, like a free eBook or coupon.

It is important to begin building your email list as soon as your website goes live. When the time comes to officially launch your startup, you should have a decent amount of contacts.

One piece of advice: never purchase an email list. The difference between buying a list and building one organically is that people who willingly provide you with their email address *want* to hear from your business. The people represented on a purchased list may or may not be interested in your business and digital content.

Conclusion

I hope you are now ready to take some massive action towards making your business goals a reality.

Don't forget to be creative, determined, always willing to follow your dreams, take calculated risks and be able to plan and delegate. There are many industries in the world in which you can create a startup business. Depending on the idea, some startups require little to no capital and others require a hefty investment. Since there are many industries to choose from, it is important to research your idea fully to establish whether there is a demand and whether it is financially feasible.

It is helpful to perform some market research before you are fully settled on a startup idea is well. With the information you gather from your research, you can begin to develop an ideal customer profile to define your target audience. Identifying your target audience early on is important for knowing how to market your products and services, how to attract customers to your business and how to eventually build brand awareness and a solid marketing strategy and plan.

Once you have secured a feasible idea and have done proper market research, the next step is to begin researching lawyers and accountants who will be able to guide you along the journey. Getting into business is very complex. There are many business and tax laws that first-time entrepreneurs may not know about and having an experienced lawyer and accountant can help you easily navigate those waters. A lawyer can also help you get set up with a legal structure that best suits your startup, which can make a big difference in paying taxes and liability protection.

Remember that when it's time to choose a name for your startup, you'll want something that is strong, powerful, easy to remember and relevant to your industry. You will also want to purchase a domain name and create multiple social media pages with your business name to begin building brand awareness. Before you settle on your business name, ensure that it is not already in use or too close to an existing business then asks some friends what they think of the name.

After selecting a name, you can begin building your brand and marketing strategy. Your marketing strategy should identify the message that you want to send to your target audience and also include your short term and long term marketing goals. Once you have a marketing strategy in place, you can begin to develop your marketing plan, which you can use to make your marketing strategy actionable. A complete marketing plan should include a brief description of the marketing challenge you face, an overview of your 4 P's, a SWOT Analysis and a summary of what marketing resources you will use to communicate with your target audience. A brand strategy is what enables consumers to differentiate your product from a similar or generic product. Don't forget about using the power of customer service to captivate your customers and stand out from your competition. Customer service is not limited to after a customer has an issue but begins as soon as your customer walks through your doors or comes across your website, social media page, etc.

Before your launch you may need to select your location of operation. There are many factors that are a part of picking the physical location of your business such as proximity to your customers, proximity to your suppliers, space size, whether it fits into your budget, whether it is zoned for business, visibility and safety. Remember that some startups, depending on their nature, may not need a permanent location at all! Keep in mind that you will also need to build and develop your team before you launch as well. While many large and established companies have positions such as CEO, CFO and President, it is important for startups to simply figure out what kind of positions they need at the beginning, fill them and then create more positions as the company grows.

A business mentor who can guide you in the direction you want to go is also very helpful. One of the best decisions I ever mad when going into a new business was to hire an experienced coach to help me on the way. I really can't recommend this enough. All the great teachers recommend this and I ignored their advice for years. Finally, after hearing this advice for like the hundredth time I decided to stop going alone and get a coach. One of the best decisions I ever made!

Finally, you must ensure that you have a financial plan for your startup business. While you will not have any solid data to work with at the beginning, you can create a 3-year sales forecast by researching similar businesses in your industry and seeking help from an experienced mentor. Additionally, it is important to create an expense list to help you maneuver your budget. An income statement, balance sheet and cash flow statement can help you manage your business finances.

Once you have launched your startup and are in business for at least 3 years, you and your team can begin to think about expanding and becoming a leader in your industry!

I wish you the best of luck on your journey! Now go ahead and take some massive action while you are motivated. Fortune favors the brave.

Thanks for reading.

If this book helped you or someone you know then be sure to leave a nice review as soon as is convenient for you, it would be greatly appreciated. For more great knowledge of the world, be sure to check out my other books.

My Other Books

Be sure to check out my author page at:

USA: https://www.amazon.com/author/susanhollister

UK: http://amzn.to/2qiEzA9

Or simply type my name into the search bar: Susan Hollister

Thank You

www.ingramcontent.com/pod-product-compliance
Lightning Source LLC
Chambersburg PA
CBHW082336220526
45470CB00008B/2534